T0331141

Enterprise Alignment and Results

Thinking Systemically and Creating Constancy of Purpose and Value for the Customer

Enterprise Alignment and Results

Thinking Systemically and Creating Constancy of Purpose and Value for the Customer

Edited by
Chris Butterworth

Routledge
Taylor & Francis Group

A PRODUCTIVITY PRESS BOOK

First edition published in 2019
by Routledge/Productivity Press
52 Vanderbilt Avenue, 11th Floor, New York, NY 10017
2 Park Square, Milton Park, Abingdon, Oxon OX14 4RN, UK

Printed on acid-free paper

International Standard Book Number-13: 978-0-367-20150-0 (Hardback)
International Standard Book Number-13: 978-0-367-20152-4 (eBook)

Visit the Taylor & Francis Web site at
http://www.taylorandfrancis.com

To Sandie, my wife and friend of over thirty years,

and our wonderful daughter Elle.

Contents

Acknowledgments

It would be impossible to name everyone who deserves naming here without doubling the size of this book. I would like to thank everyone I have met over the years who has generously shared their knowledge and experience and helped me to learn. In particular, Professor Peter Hines and all the team at S A Partners, Morgan Jones, Brenton Harder, Louis Sylvester, Richard Steel, Adam Bentley, Dan Bowes, Ron Harper, Kim Gallant, John Shapcott, and Frank Koentgen, who have all generously contributed case studies to this book. My thanks also to Mark Baker, Bruce Hamilton, and Jose Francisco Ramirez Resendiz, who have shared examples. All the team at the Shingo Institute deserve a mention and I would like to thank them for giving me the opportunity to share some of the things I have learned.

I am sure every reader will find opportunities to deepen their knowledge and apply continuous improvement to the learnings in this book. I encourage this and hope you will share your insights on the Shingo Institute blog.

Editor

Chris Butterworth has been with S A Partners for nearly twenty years. Prior to this, he had many years' experience of operating at senior management positions in several multinational organizations, including JCB, Jaguar, and Corus. He was part of the team that set up and ran one of the earliest Lean factories in the UK in the early 1990s. He was the overall program manager for the work with Cogent Power described in the Shingo Publication Award recipient book *Staying Lean*, and has spoken on the topic of "Lean Thinking" at many international conferences. He has published papers on Lean Thinking in various journals and in 2017 co-authored the widely acclaimed book *4+1: Embedding a Culture of Continuous Improvement in Financial Services*, which is based on a case study from a Shingo Silver Medallion recipient team at the Commonwealth Bank of Australia, as well as the approach taken at the Bank of New York Mellon.

He facilitates Lean Thinking and Shingo workshops for executive management teams globally and is a certified Shingo Institute Facilitator and examiner. In 2014, he was honored to be awarded Best New Speaker of the Year (TEC: The Executive Connection) for his executive talk on Lean Thinking.

Chris lives in Australia, and when he is not on the beach or walking the coast paths, he spends his time writing and learning about continuous improvement from all the people he has the pleasure of meeting in his job.

Foreword

As Executive Director of the Shingo Institute, it is my privilege to visit dozens and dozens of great organizations every year—sometimes as a Shingo examiner, sometimes with a study tour, and sometimes because these organizations invite me. The vast majority of these organizations are trying hard to follow the guiding principles of the *Shingo Model*™, and as such, these are some of the best-performing companies in the world.

Despite these organizations being top performers, many of them still struggle with bringing their organizations into alignment. When we developed the *Shingo Model*, we articulated three different principles to help organizations develop alignment:

- Create Constancy of Purpose
- Think Systemically
- Create Value for the Customer

CONSTANCY OF PURPOSE

When we developed the *Shingo Model*, we borrowed heavily from the best thinkers who have influenced the operational excellence movement. In the case of this principle, we borrowed the wording of the principle from Dr. W. Edwards Deming. The first point of Deming's 14 points is, as Deming said:

> Create constancy of purpose toward improvement of product and service, with the aim to become competitive, stay in business, and to provide jobs.*

A few years ago, the Shingo Institute developed a survey tool known as Insight. Insight is designed to help us understand better what behaviors are occurring in an organization, and also what factors are causing those behaviors. One of the initial findings from the research data suggests that

---

* Deming, W. E. Dr. Deming's 14 Points of Management. The W. Edwards Deming Institute, 2018. Available at https://deming.org/explore/fourteen-points.

the single most important principle in driving ideal behaviors is whether or not organization members understand and agree with the purpose of the organization.*

On most visits to organizations, I often ask people to tell me about the most recent improvement idea they submitted that was implemented. Typically, people are excited to tell me. This is a clear sign that these people are engaged and proud of the improvements they are driving. Unfortunately, more often than not, the conversation goes something like the following interview I documented with a line operator in a factory which applied for the Shingo Prize:

Me: "Please tell me about the most recent improvement idea you implemented."

Machine Operator: "I would love to. See this process right here? We used to do this process by (*names the steps and demonstrates the actions*). I thought of a better way by doing this (*demonstrates new steps and demonstrates the actions*). As a result of this change, we eliminated these two steps."

Me: "So this resulted in a productivity improvement?"

Machine Operator: "Yes. We improved the process productivity by about 15%. I'm able to produce more parts in the same amount of time."

Me: (*pointing to a nearby wall where the six plant goals for the year are listed—none of which include productivity improvements*) "So how does this tie in to the plant goals?"

Machine Operator: "Um ... I don't know."

Me: "What has been the impact of your productivity improvement? How has it impacted the overall performance of the line?"

Machine Operator: "I don't know that either."

I then checked with the next step in the process and discovered that the overproduction created additional work-in-process inventory.

Too often, as in this case, I see improvements that are a waste at best, and may even cause more waste—such as increased WIP inventory—because they are not aligned with the purpose and goals of the organization.

---

* Mumford, T. Cultural Strata Effects: How lean culture drivers of engagement vary by employees' level in the organization. Shingo European Conference, December 2, 2016, Copenhagen, Denmark.

Let me contrast that experience with my experiences with a company that demonstrates outstanding alignment of thinking and behaviors—a company called Autoliv. Autoliv produces air bags for automobiles. Autoliv is one of the best in the world at unifying people in the organization around a constant purpose, which they summarize in their motto of "We save lives."

I have visited Autoliv facilities dozens of times. Each time I visit, I test everyone I can with the same inquiry as above: "Please tell me about the most recent improvement idea you implemented." Every time I have made this inquiry, the person has tied the improvement back to "We save lives." Let me give an example of a typical conversation with an Autoliv team member by sharing an actual conversation with an internal accountant:

Me: "Please tell me about the most recent improvement idea you implemented."

Autoliv Accountant: "I would love to." The accountant proceeded to describe an accounting practice change that led to a decrease in work-in-process inventory (WIP). The accountant then described the amount of cash freed up by WIP reduction. The accountant then described how the freed-up cash was invested back into research and development to fund some research into a safer air bag technology Autoliv was developing. Then she stated, "This new technology will help save lives."

I was dumbstruck. Wow!

Dr. Shigeo Shingo, our namesake, described this process of how achieving one purpose becomes the means to achieve a higher purpose, and then that higher purpose becomes the means to achieve an even higher purpose, etc.

> We must learn to think of making progress as moving toward goals, because goals often become means at a higher level. When we think about a goal, we are really considering the means toward an even higher-order goal. …
>
> Goals and means trade places with one another in a chain, and the means or measures we choose will vary considerably depending upon what level of goal we recognize*

---

* Shingo, S. *The Sayings of Shigeo Shingo: Key Strategies for Plant Improvement.* Cambridge, MA: Productivity Press, 1987.

This process of converting goals into means to achieve higher-purpose goals has been described by noted scholars Professor Gerald Nadler and Professor Shozo Hibino as "purpose expansion."* I was amazed at how eloquently a staff accountant at Autoliv gave such a perfect description of "purpose expansion."

Our goal in including "Create Constancy of Purpose" in the *Shingo Model* is to encourage all organizations to align and unify everyone in the organization around a higher goal and purpose.

THINK SYSTEMICALLY

The machine operator in the first example did not understand the impact his productivity "improvement" made on the rest of the production line. Not only did the operator not understand the goals of the plant, but he had not yet learned to think systemically. This is a difficult principle to understand for some people—until it dawns on them. It seems we all must have our own "Aha!" moment when we see the overall system.

I remember my own personal struggle to understand this principle. My "Aha!" moment came when I heard a speech given by the person often credited to be the father of systemic thinking, Professor Russell Ackoff. In the speech, Professor Ackoff demonstrated systemic thinking by asking us to imagine that a group of engineers gathered all the cars produced throughout the world into one single location. The engineers then tested the cars to determine which car has the best brakes, which car has the best steering, which car has the best engine, which car has the best suspension, etc. They then took these best parts off of each car and put them altogether to make *the* best car. Professor Ackoff then asked, "What do you have?" He answered his own question, "Nothing. You don't even have a car!" He then asked, "Why?" And then answered his own question again, "Because the pieces don't fit!" Systemic thinking is about how all the pieces fit together.

Extending this analogy and applying it to the improvement efforts within organizations, the equivalent in an improvement effort would be like improving an engine so that the car can run faster, but not considering

---

* Hibino, S. and Nadler, G. *Breakthrough Thinking: The Seven Principles of Creative Problem Solving.* Rocklin, CA: Prima Publishing, 1998.

the impact speed might have on the brakes or the suspension. Too often I see improvements that don't improve the performance of the organization as a whole, and even sometimes cause a problem somewhere else. All improvement efforts should improve the performance of the organization as a whole.

CREATE VALUE FOR *ALL* CUSTOMERS

Who is the customer? All people agree that the customer is the person/organization currently giving your organization money to purchase a good or a service. What about people who might purchase that good or service in the future? Are the only customers of a hospital the patients who are having surgery or being treated in the hospital today? Of course not. What about people who must "buy-in" to the purpose and mission of the organization, i.e., its employees? Are they a different type of customer? What about people who invest in the organization, i.e., its shareholders? Are they a different type of customer? And what about people who are affected by the company, i.e., its employees' families and the community at large? In our world of instant news and social media, all of these stakeholders must be considered "customers." That is the view I take at the Shingo Institute.

In the *Shingo Model*, we define culture as the accumulation of all behaviors of the people in an organization. Formerly, an organization might have been able to build an internal culture and a separate, perhaps different, external brand image. Good research on the impact of instant news and social media demonstrates that the wall between brand and culture doesn't exist anymore. You are your brand and your brand is you. The world is increasingly transparent.

So now one might also say that the accumulation of all the behaviors is also the brand of the organization. And, increasingly, our transparent world is leading to customers finding value not just in the product or service being provided, but also in working with people who create value for them—in other words, people with the right behaviors/culture/brand who help make them better. Customers may think, "You may not have the best product yet, but you are going to provide us with the most value over time."

CONCLUSION

This book, and the associated ENTERPRISE ALIGNMENT & RESULTS workshop, are designed to help organizations make improvements that are unified around a constant purpose, that achieve goals, that improve the performance of the entire organization, and create value for all stakeholders.

Ken Snyder
Executive Director
Shingo Institute

1

Introduction

Too many organizations are failing to be competitive, not because they cannot solve problems, but because they cannot sustain the solution. They haven't realized that tradition supersedes tools, no matter how good they are. Success requires a sustainable shift in behaviors and culture, and that needs to be driven by a shift in the systems that motivate those behaviors.

Gerhard Plenert

Countless organizations have, at one time or another, begun a "Lean journey" (for a brief description of Lean, please see the end of this introduction) or they have implemented an improvement initiative of some sort. At the foundation of these initiatives are a number of tools that seem to promise exciting new results. While many organizations may initially see significant improvements, far too many of these initiatives meet disappointing ends. Leaders quickly find that Lean tools such as Six Sigma, *jidoka*, SMED, 5S, JIT, quality circles, etc. are not independently capable of effecting lasting change.

Years ago, the Shingo Institute set out on an extended study to determine the difference between short-lived successes and sustainable results. Over time, the Institute noticed a common theme: the difference between successful and unsuccessful effort is centered on the ability of an organization to ingrain into its culture timeless and universal principles rather than rely on the superficial implementation of tools and programs. These findings are confirmed time and again by nearly three decades of assessing organizational culture and performance as part of the Shingo Prize process. Since 1988, Shingo examiners have witnessed first-hand how quickly tool-based organizations decline in their ability to sustain results. On the other hand, organizations that anchor their improvement initiatives to principles experience significantly different results. This is because principles help people understand the "why" behind the "how" and the "what."

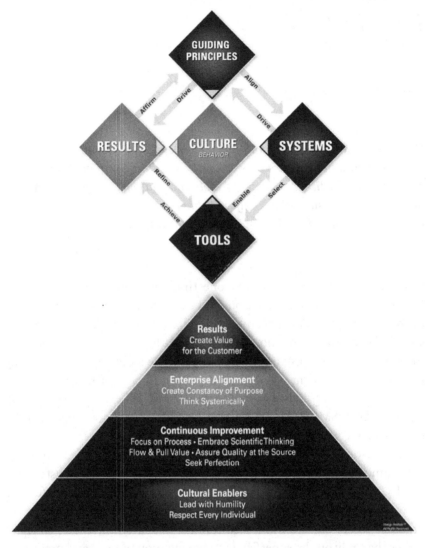

To best illustrate these findings, the Shingo Institute developed the *Shingo Model™*, the accompanying *Shingo Guiding Principles,* and the *Three Insights of Enterprise Excellence™*. The Shingo Institute offers a series of five workshops designed to help participants understand these principles and insights and to help them strive for excellence within their respective organizations. This book, *Discover Excellence: An Overview of the Shingo Model and Its Guiding Principles,* is an introduction to these five workshops.

DISCOVER EXCELLENCE (prerequisite)
Behaviors that lead to enterprise excellence

 CULTURAL ENABLERS
Behaviors that enable a culture of respect and humility

 CONTINUOUS IMPROVEMENT
Behaviors that improve a continuous flow of value

 ENTERPRISE ALIGNMENT & RESULTS
Behaviors that align people, systems, and strategy

 BUILD EXCELLENCE
Driving strategy to execution

Here is a description of the first of five workshops offered in the Shingo Institute educational series.

DISCOVER EXCELLENCE WORKSHOP

A facility-wide improvement initiative is expensive in terms of both time and money. Perhaps the most disappointing thing about them is that they often end up as temporary measures that may produce early results but are unsustainable in the long run. The unseen cost is that after they see such initiatives come and go, employees begin to see them as futile, temporary annoyances rather than the permanent improvements they are meant to be.

The *Shingo Model* begins with culture informed by operational excellence principles that lead to an understanding of what aligns systems and tools and can set any organization on a path toward enterprise excellence with sustainable continuous improvement.

The *Shingo Model* is not an additional program or another initiative to implement. Instead, it introduces *Shingo Guiding Principles* on which to anchor current initiatives. Ultimately, the *Shingo Model* informs a new way of thinking that creates the capability to consistently deliver ideal results to all stakeholders. This is enterprise excellence—the level of excellence achieved by Shingo Prize recipients.

DISCOVER EXCELLENCE is a foundational, two-day workshop that introduces the *Shingo Model,* the *Shingo Guiding Principles,* and the *Three Insights of Enterprise Excellence.* With active discussions and on-site learning at a host organization, this program is a highly interactive experience. It is designed to make learning meaningful and immediately applicable as participants learn how to release the latent potential in an organization to achieve enterprise excellence. It provides the basic understanding needed in all Shingo workshops; therefore, it is a prerequisite to the CULTURAL ENABLERS, CONTINUOUS IMPROVEMENT, and ENTERPRISE ALIGNMENT & RESULTS workshops, and concludes with the BUILD EXCELLENCE workshop.

DISCOVER participants will:

- Learn and understand the *Shingo Model.*
- Discover the *Three Insights* of Enterprise Excellence.
- Explore how the *Shingo Guiding Principles* inform ideal behaviors that lead to sustainable results.
- Understand the behavioral assessment process using a case study and on-site learning.

The additional four Shingo workshops are described as follows.

CULTURAL ENABLERS WORKSHOP

The CULTURAL ENABLERS workshop is a two-day workshop that integrates classroom and on-site experiences at a host facility to build upon the knowledge and experience gained at the DISCOVER EXCELLENCE workshop. It leads participants deeper into the *Shingo Model* by focusing on the principles identified in the Cultural Enablers dimension:

- Respect Every Individual
- Lead with Humility

Cultural Enablers principles make it possible for people in an organization to engage in the transformation journey, progress in their understanding, and, ultimately, build a culture of enterprise excellence. Enterprise excellence cannot be achieved through top-down directives or piecemeal implementation of tools. It requires a widespread organizational commitment. The CULTURAL ENABLERS workshop helps participants define ideal behaviors and the systems that drive them using behavioral benchmarks.

CONTINUOUS IMPROVEMENT WORKSHOP

The CONTINUOUS IMPROVEMENT workshop is a three-day workshop that integrates classroom and on-site experiences at a host facility to build upon the knowledge and experience gained at the DISCOVER EXCELLENCE workshop. It begins by teaching participants how to clearly define value through the eyes of customers. It continues the discussion about ideal behaviors, fundamental purpose, and behavioral benchmarks as they relate to the principles of Continuous Improvement, and takes participants deeper into the *Shingo Model* by focusing on the principles identified in the Continuous Improvement dimension:

- Seek Perfection
- Embrace Scientific Thinking
- Focus on Process
- Assure Quality at the Source
- Flow & Pull Value

This workshop deepens one's understanding of the relationship between behaviors, systems, and principles and how they drive results.

ENTERPRISE ALIGNMENT & RESULTS WORKSHOP

The ENTERPRISE ALIGNMENT & RESULTS workshop is a two-day workshop that integrates classroom and on-site experiences at a host facility to build upon the knowledge and experience gained at the DISCOVER EXCELLENCE workshop. It takes participants deeper into the *Shingo Model* by focusing on the principles identified in the Enterprise Alignment dimension and the Results dimension:

- Think Systemically
- Create Constancy of Purpose
- Create Value for the Customer

To succeed, organizations must develop management systems that align work and behaviors with principles and direction in ways that are simple, comprehensive, actionable, and standardized. Organizations must get results, and creating value for customers is ultimately accomplished through the effective alignment of every value stream in an organization. The ENTERPRISE ALIGNMENT & RESULTS workshop continues the discussion around defining ideal behaviors and the systems that drive them, understanding fundamental beliefs, and using behavioral benchmarks.

BUILD EXCELLENCE WORKSHOP

The BUILD EXCELLENCE workshop is the two-day capstone workshop that integrates classroom and on-site experiences at a host facility to solidify the knowledge and experience gained from the previous four Shingo workshops. BUILD EXCELLENCE demonstrates the integrated execution of systems that drive behavior toward the ideal as informed by the principles in the *Shingo Model*. The workshop helps to develop a structured approach to execute a cultural transformation. It builds upon a foundation of principles, using tools that already exist within many organizations. It teaches participants how to build systems that drive behavior, which will consistently deliver desired results.

In this final Shingo workshop, participants will:

- Design or create a system, guided by the *Shingo Model*, that changes behaviors to close gaps and drives results closer to organizational goals and purpose.
- Answer the question: "How do I get everyone on board?"
- Build on the principles of enterprise excellence.
- Understand the relationship between behaviors, systems, principles, and how they drive results.
- Learn how key behavioral indicators (KBIs) drive key performance indicators (KPIs), and how this leads to excellent results.
- Use Go & Observe to understand the practical application of the *Shingo Guiding Principles.*

With this understanding of what this book is all about, the reader can now take the first of many steps toward enterprise excellence.

DEFINITION OF LEAN

The term "Lean" was first adopted by authors James P. Womack, Daniel T. Jones, and Daniel Roos in *The Machine That Changed the World: The Story of Lean Production*. They describe Lean as manufacturing systems that are based on the principles employed in the Toyota Production System (TPS). Quoting them,

> Lean ... is 'lean' because it uses less of everything compared with mass production—half the human effort in the factory, half the manufacturing space, half the investment in tools, half the engineering hours to develop a new product in half the time. Also, it requires keeping far less than half the inventory on site, results in many fewer defects, and produces a greater and ever growing variety of products.*

Lean's philosophy has evolved through numerous iterations. It stresses the maximization of customer value while simultaneously minimizing waste. Lean's goal is the creation of increased value for customers while simultaneously utilizing fewer resources. To accomplish this, Lean utilized a plethora of tools (over 100) to optimize the flow of products and services throughout an entire value stream as they horizontally flow through an organization. However, Lean does not capture the focus on cultural shift, which was a necessary part of the original TPS, and which the Shingo Institute attempts to restore. The Shingo Institute uses Lean in the meaning that was intended when it was first coined by Womack, Jones, and Roos.

---

* Womack, J. P. et al. *The Machine That Changed the World: The Story of Lean Production—Toyota's Secret Weapon in the Global Car Wars That Is Now Revolutionizing World Industry*. New York, NY: Simon & Schuster, Inc., 1990, p. 14.

2

The Dimensions

We have to grasp not only the know-how but also the know why.

Shigeo Shingo*

To succeed, organizations must develop management systems that align work and behaviors with principles and direction in ways that are simple, comprehensive, actionable, and standardized. Organizations must get results and creating value for customers is ultimately accomplished through the effective alignment of every value stream in an organization. Understanding enterprise alignment means having an unwavering clarity about why the organization exists, where it is going, and how it will get there. This enables people to align their actions, as well as to innovate, adapt, and take risks with greater confidence. This is the "True North," the vision, mission, and values of the enterprise.

The Shingo Institute has created a two-day workshop, ENTERPRISE ALIGNMENT & RESULTS—often referred to as the "Align" workshop—that integrates classroom and on-site experiences at a host facility to build upon the knowledge and experience gained at the DISCOVER EXCELLENCE workshop. It takes participants deeper into the *Shingo Model* by focusing on the principles identified in the Enterprise Alignment dimension and in the Results dimension. This book is intended to supplement the Align workshop and also be useful as a stand-alone resource, as it contains many more examples and case studies than time allows for in the workshop.

Although most readers will already be familiar with the *Shingo Model* shown in Figure 2.1, here is a quick reminder of the key points.

---

* Shingo, S. *The Sayings of Shigeo Shingo: Key Strategies for Plant Improvement.* Cambridge, MA: Productivity Press, 1987.

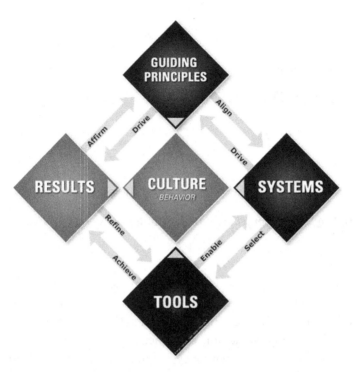

FIGURE 2.1
The *Shingo Model.*

On the left is Results, which is the reason for the existence of any enterprise. At the bottom is Tools, which is identified as the mechanisms used to accomplish the desired results. The arrows between Results and Tools stress that tools help achieve results, and as the results that one tries to achieve change, this may in turn cause a refinement of the tools that are used, either by selecting a different set of tools or by using an existing set of tools in a different way.

Moving to the right side of the figure, we see Systems. It is systems that drive behavior, which in turn reflects on the culture of an enterprise. In the *Shingo Model*, the culture is defined as the accumulation of all the behaviors in the organization. Between Tools and Systems are arrows that show that tools are used to enable and support the systems, and that systems, just like results, define and select the tools that are utilized.

Continuing this journey around the *Shingo Model*, the next box encountered is the Guiding Principles. Guiding principles are the substance which supports the purpose and the evidence of a culture.

Guiding principles inform ideal behavior. Between Systems and Guiding Principles are arrows which show graphically the interconnectedness between these two boxes. Guiding principles are the foundation used to align systems toward driving behavior closer and closer to ideal behavior.

The arrows that connect Results and Guiding Principles show that results affirm a solid foundation of guiding principles and that one needs to adhere to those principles. In turn, the guiding principles, through systems and tools, drive one toward the ideal results that one is attempting to achieve. Guiding principles are the foundation which dictate the consequences or results.

The last box in this figure, the one in the center which connects all the others, is Culture. Culture, as supported by and as manifested in behaviors, finds itself as the center-point in the development of enterprise excellence.

The *Shingo Guiding Principles* are broken into four logical groups or "Dimensions." These are shown in Figure 2.2 below.

The focus of this book is the Enterprise Alignment and Results dimensions at the top of the pyramid. The Enterprise Alignment dimension focuses on the purpose of the enterprise, and its two principles strike at the heart of an aligned, enterprise-wide purpose within the organization that everyone believes in and proactively supports. Within the Results dimension there is only one principle, and that is a focus on creating value for the customer.

The ENTERPRISE ALIGNMENT & RESULTS workshop continues the discussion around defining ideal behaviors and the systems that drive them,

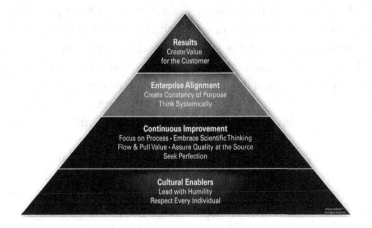

FIGURE 2.2
The *Shingo Model* dimensions and principles.

understanding fundamental truths, and using behavioral benchmarks. The workshop's primary learning objectives are to ensure that delegates:

- Understand the *Shingo Model* dimensions of Enterprise Alignment and Results
- Strengthen understanding of the relationship between behaviors, systems, and principles
- Learn how systems and behaviors drive results
- Understand the behavioral benchmarks behind the principles:
  - Create Constancy of Purpose
  - Think Systemically
  - Create Value for the Customer

In the editor's experience, senior leaders can often be heard expressing frustration that people in their organizations just "don't get the strategy," even when they have tried to communicate it several times. Communication is not enough to truly deploy strategy. Instead, organizations need to embed the principles of Think Systemically and Create a Constancy of Purpose. The following chapters explore how to bring these principles to life in any organization.

Here are some testimonials that successful enterprise excellence companies have made about Enterprise Alignment:

Alignment is when all handoffs in an organization occur properly and everybody sees the next person along the way in producing a good or service as their customer, so that you're in sync with each other and handoffs occur so that the organization operates as a system. We see integration as the next step as it's really going from alignment to integration, so there is concurrent planning, concurrent operations, and the whole is more than the sum of the parts.

Harry Hertz, *Director Emeritus,*
Performance Excellence, Baldrige, Gaithersburg, MD, US

It touches every part of the enterprise, your manufacturing operations, your office, your administrative-type functions, HR, IT, and finance. And really, it ties everything together as it relates to constancy of purpose, alignment of objectives from top to bottom. And if your organization is aligned in this manner, then you're driving these principles in your enterprise and you'll see this top to bottom.

Tony Hayes, *Director of Continuous Improvement,*
Haworth, Grand Rapids, MI, US

The two principles that underpin Enterprise Alignment, Think Systemically, and Create a Constancy of Purpose, are summarized below:

THINK SYSTEMICALLY

Simply put, what happens here either improves or is detrimental to what happens in other parts of the process. Thinking systemically means looking at the big picture. Through understanding the relationships and interconnectedness within and between systems, one is able to have better discussions and make improvements. Everything is connected, and the better one understands this connection, the better they are able to make changes that improve the system.

CREATE CONSTANCY OF PURPOSE

This principle focuses on creating unity. An unwavering clarity of why the organization exists, where it is going, and how it will get there enables people to align their actions, as well as to innovate, adapt, and take risks with greater confidence. This principle requires a methodology for communicating company information to every employee, including goals and metrics.

One example of an organization that demonstrates Enterprise Alignment is Shingo Silver Medallion recipient Barnes Aerospace Ogden. Barnes manufactures large fabrications for the aerospace industry and describes themselves as a "one stop shop," in that they perform hot forming, superplastic forming, cold forming, mechanical assembly, welding, coating, heat-treating, and brazing in-house. They have changed their visual factory to support the principle of Constancy of Purpose by making it clear to every team and every individual every day whether they are winning or losing against key goals. They have embraced the principle of Think Systemically and have focused on breaking down silos and removing any "us and them" across the workforce. Barnes employees describe how, after adopting the *Shingo Model*, they now proactively focus on being more collaborative, with one associate describing how they now look continuously for ways to keep their coworkers happy with any interaction. "We have moved from a 'having to' culture to a 'wanting to' culture, with everyone taking pride in their work." These are typical examples of the impact of applying the Enterprise Alignment principles.

It is intended that this book will help to further embed the understanding of these principles. As there is, however, always far more to learn, discuss, and experience than one could ever manage to express and include in written form, the Shingo Institute invites the reader to further their education by exploring additional avenues of education. The Shingo Institute has a wide array of licensed affiliates who can bring years of experience and expertise to clients. They are located throughout the world and are available to support those on their journey, in their own country, and in their own language. To learn more about each of the affiliates, the reader should visit shingo.org/affiliates and contact the affiliate that best matches their needs. In addition, the Shingo Institute offers private workshops for organizations upon request. These in-house workshops are tailored so that learning is specifically centered and focused on an individual organization's culture. Licensed affiliates are often available to facilitate workshops on-site and, with years of consulting experience in various industries, can assist those with specific challenges.

3

Think Systemically

Many improvement philosophies and techniques advocated in the past address only parts or aspects of a problem and have failed to be comprehensive and systematic. I propose a scientific approach to thinking through problems (STM) that combines these various philosophies and techniques in a systematic way.

Shigeo Shingo*

Dictionary definition of systemic: of or affecting the entire organism or system.

Systemic thinking is the principle that unifies all the other principles of operational excellence and enables organizations to sustain their culture of continuous improvement and to develop a constancy of purpose. Systemic thinking requires organizations to both analyze and synthesize.

Analysis, or convergent thinking, is focused on taking things apart to see what can be learned from the various components. We call this "looking into things." Convergent thinking is what leads us to focus on the "how." Synthesis, or divergent thinking, is focused on seeing how things might work together. We call this "looking out of things." Divergent thinking is what leads us to focus on the "why." Enterprise excellence requires both convergent and divergent thinking.

Leaders realize that the impact of synergy—how things work together— is far greater than the sum of the parts. As managers design and align systems with correct principles, they must shift from thinking purely analytically to thinking systemically. As managers move into systemic thinking, the full value of operational excellence is realized across the

---

* Shingo, S. *The Sayings of Shigeo Shingo: Key Strategies for Plant Improvement.* Cambridge, MA: Productivity Press, 1987.

organization, the enterprise, and, ultimately, the entire value chain. As associates adopt systemic thinking practices, they gain the necessary perspective to safely initiate improvement projects on their own. Ultimately, this understanding is what allows improvement efforts to transition from being solely top-down to more of a grassroots effort. By understanding the relationships and interconnectedness within a system, people can make better decisions and improvements that align with desired outcomes. As Peter Senge reminds us:

> Business and human endeavors are systems ... we tend to focus on snapshots of isolated parts of the system and wonder why our deepest problems never get solved.*

As Shaun Barker, Assistant Executive Director at the Shingo Institute, states:

> In order to improve the whole system ... we need to understand the connectedness between people and processes. Crosstraining is a good example—it builds a deeper understanding for people about the whole system and they begin to think differently about what they do because they now a have connection with people upstream and downstream.

One example the editor was involved in many years ago illustrates this well. Several trucks arrived one morning at the factory with very large coils of material. The goods receiving team leader explained to the editor that there were three trucks waiting in the dock that he couldn't unload. The editor went with him to understand the issue and it was clear the coils were all over 18 tons, while the maximum weight limit that the crane in receiving could safely handle was 15 tons. The drivers refused to leave, as they had been told the material had to be delivered that day. The editor went to see the purchasing manager.

Editor: "Hi, Bill. Do you know anything about a change in coil size from [xxx]?"

Bill: "Oh, yes. Great, they've started to arrive already. I got a fantastic deal on those. Did you know that by agreeing to 18-ton coils instead of the 15-ton coils we used to buy we can get a big discount?"

---

* Senge, P. M. *The Fifth Discipline: The Art and Practice of the Learning Organization.* New York, NY: Doubleday/Currency, 1990.

Editor: "No, I didn't, and great to see that you're looking after the costs.
There's just one issue though."
Bill: "What's that?"
Editor: "We've got three trucks outside from [xxx] that we can't unload
because the crane isn't rated to lift anything heavier than 15 tons."

Unfortunately, the material could not be used and had to be returned to the supplier for costly rework to split them into weights that the crane could handle. The purchasing manager genuinely believed he had done a great job reducing cost and was striving to achieve his departmental target on annual savings. However, because the decision had been made without understanding the impact on the whole process, the reality was that costs actually increased due to extra transportation and rework. Had, for example, a cross-functional team been involved in the decision-making process, the idea to buy bigger coils would have been rejected without any cost being incurred.

Systemic thinking is also reflected in one of Shigeo Shingo's teachings with regard to embedding quality in the process. One of his teachings about "Zero Quality Control" is that every step in the process should have three in-built quality checks. These are not formal inspections but instead are achieved by a deep understanding of the process. A simple way to think of it is this:

Quality Check 1: I will not accept a defect. I understand exactly how
the product or data should look when I receive it. If it is not to standard, I flag this up with the person in the process before me and
we work together to understand why this has happened and address
the cause. Accepting defects creates rework and means the issue will
never get addressed.
Quality Check 2: I will not make a defect. I fully understand what the critical quality elements are for my customer and why they are important.
Quality Check 3: I will not pass on a defect. I might make a mistake, but if I
do so, I will not knowingly pass this on to the next person in the process.

IS *THINK SYSTEMICALLY* A PRINCIPLE?

In the ENTERPRISE ALIGNMENT workshop, the delegates are asked to explore the principle of Think Systemically in order to deepen their understanding. The Shingo Institute uses several criteria to help delegates

> **Think Systemically**
>
> - What could we learn about this principle from studying the systems in your organizations?
> - What are some of the current behaviors evident in your organization as they relate to this principle?
> - How have those behaviors impacted your organization's culture?
> - Think of both positive and negative behaviors?

FIGURE 3.1
Questions to Think Systemically.

explore their understanding of this principle in more detail. The reader is encouraged to think about these criteria and consider their own answers. Each of these criteria is explored in more detail below.

IS *THINK SYSTEMICALLY* UNIVERSAL?

Does Think Systemically apply to everything? It is very hard to think of any situation where thinking systemically does not apply. Isaac Newton's Third Law of Motion that "for every action there is an equal and opposite reaction" is just one illustration. If we look at the human body, it is a complex system, and it can be very dangerous to treat just one symptom without understanding the context of the whole person. As we start to understand the environment, there are countless examples of how changing one part of the system can have a positive (or often negative) impact somewhere else.

This principle applies to all walks of life. In many different areas, systemic thinking is increasingly recognized as critical to improvement. One example that helps illustrate the widespread application of this principle comes from a recent publication, *Thinking and Acting Systemically: Improving School Districts Under Pressure*.* The authors argue that thinking systemically is critical to successful improvement. They

---

* Daly, A. and Finnigan, K. *Thinking and Acting Systemically: Improving School Districts Under Pressure*. Washington, DC: American Educational Research Association, 2016.

describe key aspects of thinking systemically as "… policies that … create opportunities for collaboration, build leader capacity, and create networks of knowledge sharing …." The authors argue that the main reason past improvement attempts have not been successful is because they did not think and act systemically and instead attempted to tackle opportunities at a local school level. They conclude that focusing on "… system-wide improvement rather than focusing on school-by-school has the potential to dramatically improve educational outcomes."

So, from every walk of life there are many examples of the applicability of thinking systemically. Perhaps we should give the final word to Aristotle: "The whole is greater than the sum of the parts."

IS *THINK SYSTEMICALLY* TIMELESS?

One way to think about this is to ask, "Is there an end point where this principle ceases to apply?" In regard to Thinking Systemically, can you think of any situation where this would be the case? It was true almost 2,300 years ago when Aristotle was alive. It is true today.

DOES IT HAVE CONSEQUENCES?

Where Think Systemically is not applied, we see time and again a lot of wasted effort and negative impacts. For example, think about how many times you hear people say, "If only I'd known *x* before I did *y*." Some examples of the consequences of not applying this principle include the following:

- Frustration and low morale when people see their efforts were wasted on the wrong thing
- Excessive wasted effort working on a part of the system in isolation which does not improve the whole system and often has a detrimental impact overall
- Conflicting departmental objectives creating waste, adding to the company cost base

Where Thinking Systemically is applied, we see the opposite of all of the above, but in addition, some of the consequences are:

- Collaboration across teams and departments focused on achieving the optimum end-to-end process
- Goals and objectives aligned across the organization
- No "us and them" between different areas of the organization

The lack of Think Systemically can cause major issues, even where the objective appears straightforward. In one company, the editor worked with the CEO, who had set a target of a 10% cost reduction over the next six months for each head of department. The head of purchasing decided that the best way to achieve this would be to buy in bulk, so that he could benefit from volume discounts. His key performance metric was unit price, and this was reduced by more than 10% by buying several months' worth of inventory on major components. The head of logistics, on the other hand, was measured on the value of stock, as it was his job to manage inventory effectively. He decided that the best way to achieve 10% cost reduction was to close one of the warehouses and consolidate stock in the remaining two warehouses by undertaking a reorganization of the layout. He was able to implement this fairly quickly. When all the extra inventory started to arrive, there was nowhere to put it and a lot of money had to be spent on short-notice temporary storage facilities. The result overall was a big increase in costs.

It was not that the cost reduction objective was wrong in and of itself, but rather the way it was implemented by departments acting in isolation meant that it was never likely to be achieved. Without a systemic approach, even with the best intentions, there are likely to be negative consequences for the overall system.

WHAT HAPPENS WHEN THIS PRINCIPLE IS OBSERVED?

In other words, think about what you would see in organizations where Think Systemically is being applied. For example, it is highly likely that you will be able to observe some of the following:

- Cross-functional teamwork and widespread collaboration
- People working together to understand each other's roles and how they contribute to the whole system

- People talking about the system or the process rather than their department
- People can explain how what they do contributes to the whole system

Professor Peter Hines provides a light-hearted, but insightful, contribution in helping to understand this principle:

What Would Happen If ...?

"Think for a minute:

- What would happen if you went to the supermarket but forgot to pick up the kids from school?
- What would happen if you bought a round of drinks in a bar for all but one of your party?
- What would happen if you booked your vacation hotel but did not book the flight to get there?

Clearly, in each case you might be embarrassed, frustrated, and/or an inconvenience to others. You would probably also incur a lot of waste and excess cost. Indeed, your less-than-ideal behavior would be a big problem.

Now let's think about the work situation:

- What would happen if you went on a gemba walk but forgot to talk to local team members at their workstation or visual management board?
- What would happen if you communicated with the day shift but not the night shift about an important change in your business?
- What would happen if you received a flat order profile from your customers but passed on a highly variable order pattern to your suppliers?

Although we may not realize it when we do these things, the outcome is likely to be pretty much the same as the first three home-based examples. These less than ideal work behaviors are caused partly through carelessness but are probably more likely because we have not been thinking systemically. Indeed, they almost certainly point to failures to define, design, implement, and sustain effective systems in the organization, such as leader standard work, communications, and supply chain integration.

So, what should we do? Well to start with, we should work to define the key systems within our organization and its wider supply chain. Second, we should review how these work from a technical point of view, but more importantly from a behavioral point of view. Third, we should prioritize improvement activity by systems based on the importance of the system and how far current practices differ from the ideal. Fourth, we should ensure we develop a discipline to maintain and further improve these systems.

Sounds easy, but these are some of the hard yards on your enterprise excellence journey. Oh, and if you succeed, you may even learn how to avoid the first three home-based problems!"[*]

IS IT RELEVANT TO OPERATIONAL EXCELLENCE?

To quote W. Edwards Deming, "A bad system will beat a good person every time."[†] Operational excellence needs to ensure that point solutions do not put a fix in one part of the system that is detrimental to the performance of the whole, either from the employees' or the customers' perspectives.

Any organization that does not think systemically about improvement runs the very real risk of making an apparent improvement to one part of the system that actually makes either performance, customer, or employee experience (and often all three) worse overall. Without systemic thinking, the claimed benefits are often illusionary, and there is a risk of damaging the credibility of any enterprise excellence initiative. Russell Lincoln Ackoff summed this up nicely:

> Managers are not confronted with problems that are independent of each other, but with dynamic situations that consist of complex systems of changing problems that interact with each other. I call such situations messes. Problems are extracted from messes by analysis. Managers do not solve problems, they manage messes.[‡]

---

[*] Hines, P. What Would Happen If …? *The Shingo Blog*, April 15, 2015. Available at https://blog.shingo.org/2015/04/what-would-happen-if/.

[†] Deming, W. E. W. Edwards Deming Quotes. *The W. Edwards Deming Institute*, 2018. Available at http://quotes.deming.org/authors/W._Edwards_Deming/quote/10091.

[‡] Ackoff, R. L. The future of operational research is past. *The Journal of the Operational Research Society*, 1979. 30: 93–104.

HOW DOES IT APPLY?

A great example of the application of Thinking Systemically is provided by J. Francisco Ramirez:

The best decisions are made when there is awareness and knowledge of the different elements of a system, as well as how these elements are interconnected and what the outputs of the system are.

Systemic thinking is a *Shingo Guiding Principle* that ties together all other principles. Thinking systemically improves understanding by learning to see the system as a whole, including elements sometimes called sub-systems. In reality, most things are connected to something else in an environment that is constantly changing.

A clear example of an integrated and complex system is the human body, as it is composed of different sub-systems such as the digestive, circulatory, or nervous systems. Each of these sub-systems performs a function while being interconnected with the others, and only its synchronized and balanced function enables the entire integrated system, the human body, to perform perfectly.

Likewise, in companies, an integrated system is composed of sub-systems that, working together, will enable the organization to achieve its best outcome. Sustainability comes through understanding the interconnections.

Understanding of the relationships and interconnections of elements of a system makes better decision-making possible and creates visibility to improvements. Systemic thinking encourages improvements to be made on the system as a whole, rather than individual components of the system, which is often where the ideas for change are initiated.

The Shingo Model itself is an example of systemic thinking. Typically, organizations go through a natural progression of learning to understand how this system works:

1. Initially, managers understand and use the tools as a way to create improvements in the business.
2. Over time, managers discover that tools are not enough and they begin to see the relationship between the tools and key systems.
3. Eventually, managers come to understand the principles and systemic thinking becomes complete when principles, systems, and tools are integrated into a perfect system.

Systemic thinking is closely related to the principle of Focus on the Process. Similarly, these two principles are closely related to key business systems such as goal alignment and gemba walks.

The leadership team of the company defines the strategies and goals in a cyclical and systematic manner. In order to achieve them successfully, it is necessary to ensure that the whole staff of the organization understands and are committed. Achieving shared goals requires good data, good analysis, and the discipline to focus on the "vital few."

The related principle of Focus on Process teaches, "Good processes make successful people." A regular and disciplined process of visiting the gemba provides the breadth of understanding required for leaders and managers to make good decisions. Seeing firsthand the interactions between related sub-systems helps in diagnosing the difference between actual and ideal behaviors and can reveal whether or not people are using the right data to manage the business and drive improvements.

The more deeply you understand the *Shingo Guiding Principles*, the more you will come to understand their connectedness. You will come to see that a few critical systems in your business touch all of these principles. This is a great example of systemic thinking.*

One way to think about Thinking Systemically is that, while Constancy of Purpose focuses on the vertical alignment of the organization, the principle of Think Systemically focuses on the horizontal alignment. Customers do not care about departments and value rarely flows through just one department in any organization. However, silos are often so strong that they prevent the efficient flow of value, and it is easy for people to lose sight of this.

Think about it. Have you ever tried to resolve an issue with a service provider and ended up being passed from one department to the next? How does it make you feel when you are told, "That's not my department, I will need to put you through to someone else?" Or, even worse, "Yes, I agree, those guys in shipping are useless, they are always messing up our orders, but I can assure you we put the right information into the system in our department."

One recent example experienced by the editor is given below. The issue that needed to be resolved was with a telephone service provider (the "Telco") who had the wrong mobile phone number stored in their customer records system. The call was made after spending ten minutes trying to resolve the issue via the online system and waiting a further seven minutes to speak to someone. The following is an abbreviated version of the transcript.

---

* Ramirez Resendiz, J. F. Beliefs and Systems Drive Behavior. *The Shingo Blog*, April 29, 2015. Available at https://blog.shingo.org/2015/04/beliefs-and-systems-drive-behavior/.

Telco: "Hello, this is [xxx]. How can I help you today?"

Customer: "Hi, there is an error with the personal records you have on file for me related to my landline and internet account."

Telco: "I'm sorry to hear that. Do you know you can just update your details online?"

Customer: "Yes, I've tried to do that, but in order for me to change that part of my profile, the system is set so I have to enter an SMS code, which it sends to my mobile. I can't do that because the mobile number it sends the code to is incorrect."

Telco: "Ok, no problem. Please tell me your account number, name, and address."

(Customer gives all these details.)

Telco: "I see this is actually a business account. My department can't process requests for business accounts. I will transfer you to the right team."

(Customer waits in another queue for three minutes for the transfer.)

Telco: "Hello, this is [xxx]. How can I help you today?"

Customer: "Hello, there is an error with the personal records you have on file for me related to my landline and internet account."

Telco: "I'm sorry to hear that. Do you know you can just update your details online?"

Customer: "Yes, as I told your colleague, I've tried to do that, but for me to change that part of my profile, the system is set so I have to enter an SMS code, which it sends to my mobile. I can't do that because the mobile number it sends the code to is incorrect."

Telco: "Ok, no problem. Please tell me your account number, name, and address."

Customer: "But I gave all these to your colleague already."

Telco: "Yes, I am sorry about that, but our security system does not pass those details through and I need to check them with you again."

Customer: "Ok." *(Gives details a second time.)*

Telco: "Thank you. I can see we have a mobile phone number on file, but I can't change that as its above my authorization level to make changes to that part of your customer profile. I will pass you on to the team that can do that."

(Customer waits in queue again.)

Telco: "Hello, this is [xxx], how can I help you today …."

Eventually, some 26 minutes later, the issue was resolved. Every single person at the Telco had been extremely helpful and had done their best to provide great customer service but the lack of Thinking Systemically in the organization as a whole meant that, despite every individual's best efforts, the customer experience was far from ideal.

Thinking Systemically is about putting the whole business view first and removing the departmental mindsets. In organizations applying this principle, people talk about "we" not "me" and actively seek collaboration across functional boundaries.

Organizations that fail to tackle existing department or silo perspectives will struggle to implement improvements effectively. To quote an old UK saying, "Turkeys don't vote for Christmas." In other words, if the changes that are being proposed threaten or challenge existing departmental fiefdoms and/or leaders' egos, they will be slowed down and often derailed. This key aspect of a Continuous Improvement culture is what Professor Doug Howardell calls "Enterprise Thinking." Howardell describes this as "the shift from functional or departmental thinking to enterprise thinking":

> Functional thinking causes people to think about their job or their depart-ment. When judging the merit of a new way of doing something, they think about the impact on themselves. This causes sub-optimization and territo-rial infighting. One of the great unseen costs for every enterprise is the cost of defending turf. When a problem occurs, people look for ways to deflect the blame. They spend hours talking, emailing, and presenting data about why it's not their fault. When an improvement is suggested, they spend even more time trying to make sure the change affects everybody but them. Enterprise thinking can only exist when everyone, from top to bottom, understands what we mean by a process—the conversion of input to out-put by applying value—and when everyone knows that all work is accom-plished by a process. Enterprise thinking means we look for the common good, not our individual or departmental good.*

One common barrier to this shift in thinking is the senior leadership team meeting structure. Often the senior leadership team meetings are reporting sessions on each area of responsibility, and success is measured by how well each part of the business is operating. In other words, each

---

* Howardell, D. Lean People for a Lean Enterprise. *The ACA Group*, 1 January, 2011. Available at www.theacagroup.com/lean-people-for-a-lean-enterprise/.

executive primarily focuses on how well their department is doing, as this is the focus of the performance measures. Changing the focus of these meetings to make the team accountable for how the business is operating as a whole and how they can collaborate and support each other often has a dramatic impact.

In one team the editor worked with, the executive team stopped reporting on department performance at each meeting and instead agreed on the high-level business Key Performance Indicators (KPIs) they would all be accountable for as a team. At the same time, they agreed on some Key Behavioral Indicators (KBIs) around how well they were working collaboratively. The tone and value of these meetings became much more positive as a result, and the change in behavior that this instigated had a significant and very positive impact on the overall culture of the business.

The language that leaders and associates use changes in organizations that embed the principle of Think Systemically. We do not hear phrases like, "Well, we've done our part—it's the guys in department x that have messed up." Instead, leaders and managers will talk about how their department can support other areas and ensure that people in their teams focus on the whole process through the eyes of the customer. They will actively encourage collaboration across departments and reinforce the fact that their team can only succeed if every team is a "winning team." This can manifest itself in several ways and these are explored in more detail below.

PROBLEM SOLVING

One of the activities that can demonstrate how well an organization is thinking systemically is the way that problem-solving activities are conducted. For example, do individuals or teams solve problems entirely in isolation and focus on solutions that work for them? They may not do this deliberately, but the absence of thinking systemically could mean that they are not aware of the risks of doing this or simply do not consider the need to involve others. Where the principle is embedded, teams will ensure they pull in people from other areas, especially areas upstream or downstream that may be impacted or could contribute to analyzing the problem and possible solutions. An example of the kind of conversation that might take place where Think Systemically is working well is given below:

Team Leader: "I would like to welcome Jim and Lisa to our problem-solving meeting. For those of you who have not met Jim, he is the team leader of team [x] in R&D, and Lisa is a member of team [x]. I invited them to our problem-solving meeting today as I thought their input would be very useful. Welcome, Jim and Lisa, and thanks for joining us."

Jim: "Hi, everyone. Many thanks for the opportunity to take part."

Lisa: "Hi, everyone. This is my first time in operations, so I'm looking forward to the session."

The team then carries out a Fishbone and 5 Whys problem-solving exercise and invites Jim and Lisa to contribute.

Jim: "It appears that one of the root causes is that you are not getting information you need from team [x] in R&D on time."

Team Leader: "Is there anything we can do to help you get this to us quicker?"

Lisa: "We didn't realize how important this particular information is and we haven't been monitoring it closely. But if you can give us visibility of deadlines one week out and update them weekly, then I think we should be able to hit them. What do you think, Jim?"

Jim: "Yes, that should work, but we need to test it out and check that it works before we can say that it will definitely fix the issues."

Team Leader: "How about Lisa and Steve from our team get together and draft up a PDCA action plan on this and we all get together to review the results in four weeks?"

Jim: "Sounds good to me. Let's go for it."

Some organizations will ensure their problem-solving system supports Think Systemically. For example, one engineering company that makes complicated braking systems has the following problem-solving process embedded: Whenever a defect or error occurs, the first question everyone is taught to ask is, "Did we follow our Standard Operating Procedure (SOP)?" If the answer is no, then the team must complete a 5 Whys analysis to identify the root cause. It cannot be done just by one or two people—the whole team must take part. If the answer is, "We think so," then this is potentially a bigger issue, as either the SOP is not understood or there is something incorrect with it. The required standard response in this case is that a cross-functional team must be formed to undertake a detailed eight-step problem-solving activity. This approach has helped to achieve zero defects with external customers for several years.

HUDDLES

How huddles are structured in terms of agenda, attendees, and participation are all very powerful indicators as to whether the organization has embedded Think Systemically. At a basic level, a huddle should have good interaction across the team that demonstrates they are thinking systemically in their own part of the process at least. However, what is more powerful is if there are specific requirements in place in the huddle system that encourage wider participation. For example:

- Leaders are required to attend a certain number of huddles outside their own area every week.
- Associates regularly attend other team huddles.
- People from other areas are encouraged and actively welcomed to the huddle.
- Internal customers and suppliers are specifically invited to take part in huddles and give feedback.

A typical conversation that might take place to encourage this could be something like this:

Leader: "How effective are the team huddles?"
Team Leader: "They are getting better, and we are now having some great discussions and getting faster resolution on a couple of issues that have been around for a while."
Leader: "Well done. That sounds great. Are there any improvements you would like to try?"
Team Leader: "We have just started having each team member take a turn at running the huddle and are getting better engagement as a result but are not sure what else we could try."
Leader: "I see you have a customer value proposition on your visual management board, which is great. Have you had any of your internal customers attend your huddles?"

Team: "No, but that's an interesting idea. I will discuss it with the team
and see what we can set up."

Leader: "Sounds good. Please let me know how it goes."

VALUE STREAM MAPPING

Value stream mapping is a very useful tool to help support Thinking
Systemically. Like many tools, its effectiveness to a large extent depends
not on *what* is done but much more on *how* it is done. The best approach
will ensure that a cross-functional team with representatives from across
the whole process will create the value stream map and analyze the map
together. The approach that will not be anywhere near as effective is to have
an external consultant come in, walk the process, and present the map to
the business. At a superficial level, both outputs will probably look very
similar, but their impact on changing the way people behave and think
systemically will be markedly different. Done well, a value stream mapping
exercise is a powerful change management tool that enables people to see
the whole process and helps them to understand how they personally
contribute and what their colleagues do. It results in a huge number of
"just do it" improvement suggestions and some significant projects, but
one of its biggest impacts is on the way people understand their role and
the impact they have on the colleagues upstream and downstream. "I had
no idea that you had to do that—if only I'd known" must be one of the
most common phrases overheard in a value stream mapping team.

THE BONUS SYSTEM

Many bonus systems are heavily weighted toward personal or departmental
achievement. While this is good for driving performance and personal
accountability for results, if it is too heavily weighted on individual parts
of the system rather than the whole, it will often result in the wrong
behaviors and a sub-optimized system. For example, one company known
to the editor managed to turn around the whole business performance
significantly by changing the senior executive bonus structure. Instead

of rewarding each departmental head for how well their department performed, the bonus was based entirely on three business level KPIs and a weighting on collaborative behavior. For example, the sales bonus was previously based on meeting a monthly sales target that had been set at the start of the year. This led to people holding back on booking sales if the monthly target had already been made, and, in "slow" months, artificially pulling forward sales to hit the target even if the deal was not quite finalized with the customer. This often resulted in last minute changes and cancellations or rework the following month once the final deal had actually been signed off. The operations team were previously bonused on the volume of output measured in tons, which led to massive inventory levels of product that was easy to make but no one had ordered, so it had to be sold off at a discount to shift it. The new bonus was based on achievement of four things:

- On-time, in-full of good quality product delivered to the customer
- Employee engagement scores
- Total inventory levels
- A peer review behavioral assessment

It was not perfect, but certainly a big improvement on the previous system, and was reviewed and changed again two years later when it had achieved the initial desired results.

There are several other ways that organizations seek to apply the principle of Thinking Systemically. One of the options is to change the emphasis of KPIs and targets so that they do not reward departmental performance, but instead reward business performance and collaboration. It may be difficult to move away entirely from departmental performance targets, but it is good practice to ensure there is also an enterprise perspective to the KPIs and targets, and that the KBIs encourage cross-departmental collaboration.

Another approach often seen to support the principle of Think Systemically is to appoint high-level process owners whose role is to oversee the end-to-end process and make the call on any perceived department conflicts or barriers that get in the way of value flowing smoothly. This can work well, provided the roles, accountabilities, and authority levels are clearly defined. Most often, in order to work successfully, it also requires a change in the KPIs used to measure the senior leaders and managers. For example, where the roles are put in place but the primary reward and recognition KPIs are still strongly departmentally focused, the roles will often fail to deliver the desired output.

An approach that some high-performing organizations have taken is to change the organizations' structure and the business KPIs to reflect customer value streams, and to appoint senior level value stream managers. The value streams are usually based on specific customer market segments and seek to align ownership and measures and targets focused on delivering customer value. While this is a big step to take, in the right context, it can have very powerful results and has been applied by several Shingo recipient organizations.

5 WHYS

While 5 Whys is a very useful tool for drilling down to the root cause of a problem simply by asking "why" to each progressive answer, it can also be used to help deepen our understanding of many different things. In the workshop, delegates are asked to apply the 5 Whys technique to each principle in order to help understand and explore its deeper meaning (see Figure 3.2).

It is useful to try and put this principle into your context. Ask yourself why this principle is important to your organization. This is a good exercise to deepen understanding of the principle and its application to your organization, and this exercise works really well if undertaken by a cross-functional team. Applying Thinking Systemically in discussing Thinking Systemically is a good start.

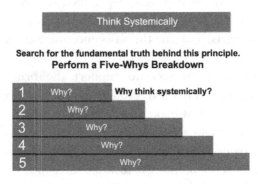

FIGURE 3.2
5 Whys to Think Systemically.

The context and thus the answers for each organization will be different but a generic example is given below.

1. Why is Thinking Systemically of value to our organization?
   Answer: Because we currently operate in strong departmental silos that we need to change.
2. Why do we need to change the department silos?
   Answer: Because we need to make sure we understand the whole process before we make decisions to change things.
3. Why do we need to make sure we understand the whole process before we make decisions to change things?
   Answer: Because if we don't, we could make one part really good but make the whole system even worse.
4. Why is this important?
   Answer: Because it's very frustrating and causes a lot of waste and issues for the customer when we do this.
5. Why is this important?
   Answer: Because when we do this, it costs us a lot of money, demotivates staff, and upsets the customer.

EXAMPLES OF IDEAL BEHAVIORS

Some examples of behaviors that we observe that demonstrate the application of the principle of Think Systemically are given here:

Think Systemically	Example Behavior
Leader	Proactively encourages collaboration across departmental boundaries
Manager	Always focuses on optimizing the end-to-end process, not their own department
Associate	Understands how their role contributes to the end-to-end process

The summary of reasons why the Shingo Institute believes that the principle of Think Systemically is important can be seen in Figure 3.3.

Think Systemically

Business Case:
Through understanding the relationships and interconnectedness within a system we are able to make better decisions and improvements.

Fundamental Truth:
As we see how and why everything is connected to, or part of, something else, it helps us to better understand, predict and control outcomes.

FIGURE 3.3
Importance of Think Systemically.

COGENT POWER CASE STUDY

The case study below from Cogent Power Inc. in Canada illustrates many aspects of Think Systemically, including the reorganization of the company into value streams with dedicated value stream managers. The case study is written by company president Ron Harper, who kindly shares some of the Cogent story and his personal insights.

Case Study: Cogent Power Inc.—Lean Story

Cogent Power Inc. (Burlington) is a subsidiary of Cogent Power Group Ltd, based in Newport, South Wales, UK. The group of companies are global suppliers of magnetic (electrical) steels and components used primarily for electrical power engineered products such as generators, motors, and transformers. The business unit is currently owned by Tata Steel Limited.

The Early Days: Learning Lean

Cogent Power started its Lean journey as part of a corporate initiative at the end of 2003. An acquisition completed in 2001 diversified the business, and it was in a ripe position for restructuring. At the time, there were ten individual businesses based in the UK, Germany, Sweden, Hungary, the United States, and Canada. A new managing director was appointed to the Cogent Power Group to restructure the business and build a strong platform for business growth and financial performance. This managing director came from the tier-one auto parts sector in Europe, and as such, his business philosophies were rooted in Lean manufacturing, with an entrepreneurial spirit. Leaders of each of the individual units were expected to learn and start to build the manufacturing platform and business structure around the basic principles of Lean. This started with five key building platforms that are still fundamental to the Cogent strategic approach today: Strategy Deployment; Value Stream Management; Lean Tools and Techniques; Extended Value Stream Perspective; and People Enabled Processes and Engagement.

Cogent worked very closely with S A Partners Consulting (Cardiff, UK) on building the basic Lean understanding and the strategy going forward. Each business appointed a dedicated Lean Coach, who was a senior leader responsible for progressing the application of Lean inside of the organization. The Lean Coaches looked after the tracking and progress against specific timelines and reported centrally to a Lean Director in addition to their local businesses, who oversaw all progress within each of the companies. Lean Coaches received three weeks of intensive training by S A Partners, providing a strong base of Lean understanding. Initial focus in each of the business units was the application of Lean tools such as 5S and its associated auditing processes. Early on, a Lean Maturity audit process was established to gauge progress at each business unit against the five platforms identified previously.

This early work spanned an 18–24-month period, and progress was made at the shop floor level in all businesses. The Lean Coach model was expanded, and shop floor level coaches were established (Lean Support Coaches). The Lean Support Coach model was put into place to start the process of gaining a platform of stability of improvement efforts and spreading awareness of the basic principles of Lean and its benefits to shop floor teams. Additionally, all leaders attended a one-week training from S A Partners on Lean Management and Leadership. The leaders and a good cross-section of the workforce were able to speak the language of Lean, understood the basic concepts and philosophies and some of the common tools, and the Lean Coaches presented the organization and the early story well. Much of the work in the first two years of the Cogent story is well-documented in the book *Staying Lean*, written by Professor Peter Hines et al.[*]

---

[*] Found, P., Griffiths, G., Harrison, R., and Hines, P. Staying Lean: Thriving, Not Just Surviving. Cardiff, UK: Lean Enterprise Research Centre, Cardiff University, 2008.

It all appeared that the business was moving in a good direction with adopting a Lean philosophy; however, there were a couple of fundamental flaws in the approach that were not clear until after this period. Through the initial two-year period, the real owners of the Lean transformation were the Lean Coaches (i.e., not the business leaders). As such, the investment in Lean was not translating into changes in behavior and culture in the organization, and no business benefits were being realized. Leaders were running the business as in the past, using some of the Lean tools as templates to present strategy and performance, and much of the focus of the transformation in the organization was on the first three elements of 5S: Sort, Set, and Shine. Additionally, it became clear that the Lean initiative did not have a clear long-term focus. It was announced that the Cogent business was not strategic for the owners (Corus Group PLC at the time) and was being put up for sale. It was later learned that this was the plan all along, in that the business was to invest in a way to make it more valuable in a divestment. Additionally, the lack of effective use of value stream mapping and the elements of creating flow did not receive any focused attention, since effective implementation of process changes to create dramatically better flow required business leader focus, attention, and support.

One Leader Wakes Up to the Opportunity

Early in the third year of work at the Burlington business, Cogent Power Inc. (CPI), the potential for significant improvement in business performance advancing Lean principles got the attention of the general manager of the company, Ron Harper. Up to this point, Ron had delegated much of the Lean work to Greg MacDougall, the company's Lean Coach and quality manager. Ron started to realize that, to make the Lean work turn into real change and business performance, a fundamental change in his mindset and approach to leading the business in a Lean thinking way was required. The approach and success of Lean was only going to realize its potential with strong leadership that set the tone for change—change to a Lean thinking mindset.

As this understanding emerged, some of the previous training, work, and organizational behavior was revisited. Middle managers (previously, a mostly ignored group) received improved training from S A Partners, and the ownership of the Lean transformation was transferred over to the business leadership team. The Lean coaches

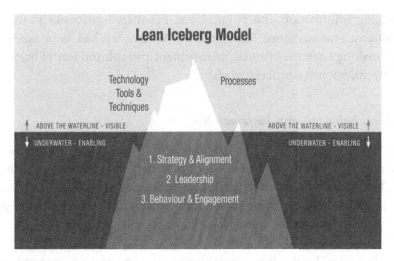

FIGURE 3.4
Lean Iceberg Model.

became supportive partners in a mentoring and coaching role. This proved to be an interesting challenge, as the Lean coaching team enjoyed owning the work and the results of the Lean initiatives. The results being achieved, however, were "above the water line" (see Figure 3.4),* and not translating into any significant business benefits. The missing link was the business and operating leaders using the Lean tools and thinking as a means to improve business and operating performance, which was only going to be achieved if the leaders took hold of the reins of the Lean transformation. This is the point at which CPI engaged with the Association of Manufacturing Excellence (AME), primarily as a learning place for the leaders and practitioners in the company to build Lean knowledge and experience.

Looking for big early wins, a Lean mapping initiative was undertaken to improve the flow of steel raw materials through the CPI process to lower work-in-process (WIP) inventory and create physical space for growth. This was a large opportunity for business improvement as well as material flow. This remains today as one of the most significant improvements in the CPI process, as WIP inventory was reduced by $6 million, generating significant cash for the business and eliminating significant process and human wastes. Some very good work through the mapping process of

---

* Found, P., Griffiths, G., Harrison, R. and Hines, P. Staying Lean: Thriving, Not Just Surviving. Cardiff, UK: Lean Enterprise Research Centre, Cardiff University, 2008.

changing information and physical and behavioral processes yielded a significant and sustained improvement. A new step had been taken to start making Lean the business management and cultural way of business at Cogent, not just a processing change.

Culture, Behavior, and Sustainability

Passing over the Keys

The next stage of progression of CPI was to start to integrate the cultural and behavioral aspects necessary for a Lean transformation and a high-performance Lean management system. Several key initiatives were put into place to help build the continuous improvement culture.

- Frontline Leadership Development: An organization change put a formal team leader structure into place to support the movement of authority and ownership to the shop floor level. This included the development of an 18-month leadership program that incorporated both hard and soft skills training for leadership. A conversion from a "supervisory" style to a coaching style was made at the shop floor leadership level.
- Employee Engagement and Accountability Training/Work: To start building the framework across the company for accountability and engagement at all levels of the organization, CPI partnered with Partners in Leadership, a San Diego-based company that specializes in creating high-performing, accountable organizations through behavioral change models and simple and effective ownership models.
- Lean Apprentice Program: A Lean apprentice program was developed that brought operating team members in from the shop floor and put them on a six-month learning and work program. They focused on kaizen and work improvement projects using Lean tools and leadership skills. They also attended leadership training similar to the frontline leadership program for improvement in communication and facilitation skills. At the end of the six months, they were either reassigned (many have become team leaders or taken on other staff responsibilities) or returned to their previous production duties. This helped the culture spread throughout the shop floor.
- Line of Sight Processes: Standardized communication and visual management processes were put into place for business and operational flow performance management and improvement.

- Stop-line Jidoka: A stop-line Jidoka process was developed, with training for all employees on "at the line" problem solving. This process included the incorporation of Andon lights, and the responsibility for problems to be solved at the shop floor level and escalated when additional resources for more complex problems emerged.
- CI Idea Program: A continuous improvement idea program was developed, which has had significant success in generating improvement ideas from all sources within the company.

Redefining Lean: Value and Waste, Not Just Waste

Part of the more holistic perspective provided at this stage shifted the focus and definition on Lean from "waste" elimination only to the broader definition that included a full perspective, including generating value for clients. This is the definition that CPI uses today for "Lean" (see Figure 3.5).

Value Stream Reorganization

This work has been done in the context of a reorganization of the company into value streams, starting in 2008. This leadership reorganization shifted the company from a functionally oriented hierarchy to a true value stream organization. Three value streams were identified, aligned with the main four product streams of the company. Each of the value streams was appointed a senior leader, and the leader designed their operational and support teams in accordance with the needs of the client and the value stream's effective flow. Previous functions such as logistics, production planning, inside sales and customer service, quality, and engineering

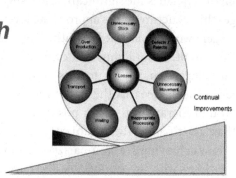

Lean Thinking is a proven path to
Profitable Growth

Driven by providing best possible cost &
Customer Value

Enabled by the ruthless and relentless elimination of
Waste

Continual Improvements

The 7 Waste of Lean Manufacturing

FIGURE 3.5
Definition of Lean.

were integrated into the value streams and reported directly to the value stream leader. In this reorganization, the three business value streams were created with an identified value stream leader, and five deployment (old terminology: "functional") areas that addressed the governance and functional needs and responsibilities of the organization. The premise and goal were, as Jim Womack identifies it, to balance the strong organizational flow through the value streams horizontally to the client, with the vertical flow of authority in the organization. Strong functional leadership and strong value stream leadership were established.

This transition had many challenges, primarily with the functional deployment leaders. The value stream leadership roles emerged into a strong business leadership role aligned with the flow of value to clients, but this process required strong mentoring and development of the new value stream leaders (who had traditionally been production-focused only). The challenge with the functional leaders was that they felt (initially) that some of their traditional power had been removed, because elements of their team were now dispatched into the value stream structure. This overall transition took several years to mature, and significant leadership training, development, and mentoring to balance the "shared ownership" model. The traditional position power orientation shifted to a personal power need to get the desired results at both the value stream and functional deployment level.

The current organization model is shown in Figure 3.6.

Holistic Leadership Framework vs. Hierarchical

The transformation into this organizational structure, and its subsequent maturity, had some significant leadership challenges. It took a few years to get this structure to the appropriate level of maturity. During the process, Cogent worked very closely with a business transformation and leadership consultant, Jump Point, and continues to work closely with them today. The biggest challenges to this transition were at the senior leadership level. The degree that the leadership team and organization were oriented around hierarchical and a position power-based culture was far greater than anticipated. The organizational and structural changes that Cogent is now achieving are summarized in Table 3.1.

Leaders who are comfortable and have been successful with a traditional hierarchical focus significantly struggled to shift to the mindset and the performance expected through the value stream structure. Through this transition, several senior leaders left the company through resignation

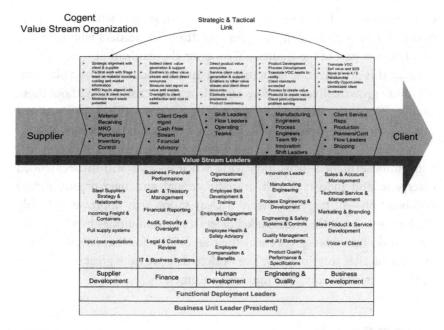

FIGURE 3.6
Cogent Value Stream Leadership Model.

TABLE 3.1

Old Structure vs. New Structure at Cogent

Old Structure and Mindset	New Structure and Mindset
Functional and positional power oriented	Holistic, cross-functional, and personal power oriented
Horizontal flow of authority	Vertical flow of value to clients and horizontal flow of authority
Internal focus	Client focus
Focus on metrics	Focus on results
Process and product development	People, process, and product development
Incremental change	Transformational change
Work process focus	Work process and behavioral focus
Manage with organizational power	Lead as if you have no power
Functional team focus	Cross-functional team focus
Improvement and problem focus for point optimization	Improvement and problem focus on holistic results
Decisions centered on leaders	Decisions centered on teams closest to the work and team leaders

or retirement, and, as such, were replaced with leaders who were able to operate in the holistic value stream structure. The leaders who left were the strongest part of the traditional functional organization.

Today this organization structure is maturing and is creating a platform for future growth, diversification, and client value creation. Without these changes, Cogent's market position would be weaker, and the organizational capacity for future growth and sustainability much more questionable.

The senior leaders of CPI believe that advancing the Lean thinking agenda, with a mindset of client focus, improving "whole systems" within the extended enterprise and industry, with cross-functional and inter-organizational collaboration—all targeted toward a clear vision that improves not only the businesses, but the wider stakeholders and communities in which they live and do business—gives them the best chance for that long-discussed and sought-after sustainability. The work to date provides great examples of "Thinking Systemically." The journey continues.

BEHAVIORAL BENCHMARKS

The Shingo Institute believes that considering what is referred to as "behavioral benchmarks" can deepen the understanding of this principle. These are intended to help us look at the principle from many different perspectives and act as a guide or reference point to help define behaviors that support this principle. It is not the intention that the application of this principle is limited to only these behavioral benchmarks, as it is important to remember that the context of every organization is unique. However, they provide a very useful basis for further discussion and exploration of the principle. The two behavioral benchmarks for Think Systemically are Optimization and Linkage, and these are explored below.

Optimization: We consider how improvements in our area need to align with improvements in the whole organization.

A company could put a top man at every position and be swallowed by a competitor with people only half as good, but who are working together.

W. Edwards Deming*

---

* Stevens, T. Dr. Deming. Management Today Does Not Know What Its Job Is (Part 2). *Industry Week*, January 17, 1994. Available at www.industryweek.com/quality/dr-deming-management-today-does-not-know-what-its-job-part-2.

It is unfortunately very easy to optimize one part of the process with the best of intentions, but cause unexpected and often unknown consequences somewhere else. The story below is a true story from an engineering company employing around one hundred people. It is a good example of what can go wrong even in a relatively small business. The company name has been disguised for confidentiality reasons.

The XYZ Widget Company

The XYZ Widget Company was experiencing a major issue with achieving On-Time In-Full (OTIF) delivery to their customers and yet at the same time had excess inventory. The combination of these two factors was having a negative impact on cashflow and the CEO decided to get a team together to map the end-to-end process from customer order to invoicing.

A value stream map of the process was constructed by a team from all areas, including operations, purchasing, finance, logistics, and stores and sales. Data was collected for each part of the process and then the team analyzed the data and the map. One area that stood out as causing a lot of noise and frustration was stock accuracy. Although stock accuracy was measured from a financial perspective each quarter, it was not a KPI that was regularly reported on and had no clear ownership. The team decided to look at this in more detail and constructed a detailed process activity map on the "goods inwards" process, as this was the start of the on-site process in terms of ensuring stock accuracy. They mapped from a vehicle arriving to the supplier being paid. The result was fascinating.

Tom, who was in charge of goods, walked an average of three kilometers per day taking delivery paperwork from the stores area up to the "in tray" in the purchasing office so it could be processed. Steve, who worked in purchasing and had multiple jobs to complete, decided that while processing this paperwork was a necessary evil, it got in the way of doing the really important stuff such as chasing down suppliers for urgent deliveries. In order to optimize his time, when he started in the role 12 months previously, he decided that the most efficient way to deal with this paperwork was to batch it all together and process it in a "blitz" every Friday afternoon when things were normally a bit quieter. This worked wonderfully well for him and dramatically reduced the amount of total time he spent processing the paperwork.

However, the negative consequences on the business were dramatic, with several things going wrong in the whole process as a result. These included:

- It could be up to a week before material that had been delivered was booked on the system. A computer system default would not let material stock go into a negative so it was not possible to record the issuing of material until it was booked on the system. This meant that Tom had to keep a separate paper record of what he had issued and then go back into the system at a later date to enter the information.
- Tom sometimes made a mistake or occasionally missed an item from his manual list, which was easy to do, and, as a result, some supplier invoices could not be paid, as there was no record of the material being received.
- Some suppliers were in dispute about not being paid and one had even suspended deliveries.
- The production planning department based plans on material that was available, and there was often heated debate between planning and production about why a job that was late was not being planned until the last minute when they could see the material sitting in the stores. The planner could not issue the plans without material being on the system. As a result, operations often started a job that was on the plan because they could and it was, in their view, the right thing to do. This created massive rework and confusion with poor visibility of what was actually being worked on and the expected completion date.
- Customers called constantly for updates and the customer service team had to hunt down people to find out what was going on.
- Tom was very frustrated.

The team did a root cause analysis, which involved both Tom and Steve as part of the team. The root cause identified was that there was no process in place for immediately booking in material as soon as it arrived on site. Initially, Steve was somewhat defensive about this, but, recognizing the impact, offered to process any documents he received within two hours, providing he could get some help with some of the other things he needed to do. Then one of the team asked Tom why he couldn't just book the receipts himself as soon as he had unloaded the truck.

"You've got to be kidding me," said Tom. "No way I've got time to do that! Have you any idea how busy I am? I am walking three kilometers a day backwards and forwards to purchasing from the stores. I am having to write everything down because I can't issue it on the system and then spend hours checking to see it's been booked in before I can enter the data in the system. I am constantly trying to track material that operations have helped themselves to because they've taken it before it's booked out and now you want me to do something else as well? No way have I got time to do that."

There were several seconds of silence as the team absorbed this and Tom calmed down. Slowly, he looked round the room and sheepishly said, "I guess if I did book the stuff myself, I wouldn't have to do any of those other things, would I?"

One of the team said, "What do you need from us to help try it out, Tom?"

"I need Steve to train me how to do it and to help out in the transfer so we can make sure everything works okay. We also need to work out what to do with the paperwork once the material is booked out."

"No problem," says Steve, "I'll get to work on that with you straight away."

Within a couple of months, OTIF had improved, stock had gone down, and Tom, Steve, and customers were much happier. Unfortunately, Tom complained that the lack of exercise meant he now needed to buy a gym membership.

Very few people will deliberately make a change that messes up the next person in the process. Most of the time this happens because there is a lack of understanding about how an improvement being planned by one person or team will impact other areas. Unless behaviors are defined and encouraged that demonstrate Think Systemically and systems are put in place that encourage these behaviors, this will continue to be an issue. As Frederick Winslow Taylor, author of *The Principles of Scientific Management*, put it:

> We can see our forests vanishing, our water-powers going to waste, our soil being carried by floods into the sea; and the end of our coal and our iron is in sight. But our larger wastes of human effort, which go on every day through such of our acts as are blundering, ill-directed, or inefficient, and which Mr. Roosevelt refers to as a lack of "national efficiency," are less visible, less tangible, and are but vaguely appreciated.*

---

* Taylor, F. W. Scientific Management, comprising *Shop Management, The Principles of Scientific Management* and Testimony Before the Special House Committee. New York, NY: Harper & Row, 1911.

Another aspect to optimization is the willingness to test out solutions to understand how they impact the whole system. Having cross-functional teams apply the Plan, Do, Check, Act approach enables the constant refinement and iteration of solutions. This allows the optimization of the solutions, as knowledge of the impact on the whole system is deepened with every cycle. This is summed up by Kate O'Neill:

> Embrace iteration as the road to improvement, but don't let that lull you into rolling out poorly-thought-out crap.*

Some examples of behaviors that we observe that demonstrate the application of this behavioral benchmark are given in Table 3.2.

Some examples of possible Key Behavioral Indicators that could be used for optimization are given below. These are not intended to be the definitive list and may not be appropriate in every organization. Rather, they are examples that can be used to help understand the concept of KBIs and inform discussion on what some might be for your own organization.

- Number of public celebrations of experimentation held each month
- Percentage of employees recognized for the efforts in improvement activities (peer nominated)
- Percentage of problem-solving activities undertaken by cross-functional teams

TABLE 3.2

Optimization Behaviors

Think Systemically: Optimization	Example Behavior
Leader	Publicly encourages and celebrates experimentation
Manager	Asks questions that encourage and recognize experimentation
Associate	Proactively involved in efforts to optimize processes

---

* O'Neill, K. *Lessons from Los Gatos: How Working at a Start-up Called Netflix Made Me a Better Entrepreneur.* Seattle, WA: Amazon Digital Services LLC, 2014.

Linkage: We know how our work impacts the work of others.
One of the reasons this is important is described neatly by Russell Ackoff:

> To manage a system effectively, you might focus on the interactions of the parts rather than their behavior taken separately.*

Linkage is about ensuring everyone in the organization knows not only their role or lists of tasks, but also how what they do fits into the wider system. They know why what they do is important and the impact it has on other parts of the system. In other words, rather than just being efficient in their tasks, they are also effective in them, as they understand the wider impact of what they do.

One story to illustrate the power of linkage and what can happen if we do not do this comes from a very large utility company. The human resource director was getting concerned about the large increase in the number of recruits required in the engineering department. It was getting so high that her team was considering recruiting someone to cope with the recruitment requirements. This seemed strange, as sales volume and activities had not increased to anywhere near the same level. Intrigued, she decided to have a chat with the engineering director to understand why all the recruitment was necessary. The conversation went something like this:

HR director: "Hi, Jim. Just wanted to discuss all the recruitment requests we are processing and understand the situation a bit more. Just wondered, what's driving the need for all these extra people?"

Engineering director: "We just can't cope with the backlog we have for checking faulty meter readings. It's been growing and growing for the last 12 months and we now have a six-month backlog based on current resources. One of the new customer service KPIs we agreed to introduce is that we will do these checks within four weeks and we are failing badly. Myself and my team are getting really stressed by it and customers are getting increasingly frustrated."

HR director: "Well, that's clearly a big issue. Do you know why we are getting this level of requests to check the meters?"

Engineering director: "That's a good question. They have been reliable for years. As far as we can tell, nothing has changed."

HR director: "When did the volume start increasing like this?"

* Crawford-Mason, C. and Dobyns, L. *Thinking about Quality: Progress, Wisdom, and the Deming Philosophy.* New York, NY: Random House Value Publishing, 1998.

Engineering director: "Umm. Now that I think about it, around the time we introduced the new set of customer service KPIs."

HR director: "Jim, something just doesn't feel right about this. How do you feel if we set up a meeting with the director of customer service and see if we can set up a cross-functional team to map the process and see what's happening? I don't think we can just keep recruiting at these rates—it's not sustainable."

Engineering director: "Ok. It's got to be worth a try."

A cross-functional team was set up to map the process, and two weeks later reported back the findings. Lots of quick wins were identified along with several longer-term improvement projects. The root cause to the main issue came as a surprise. The key metric for the customer service team was to ensure they had resolved any call from a customer in less than two minutes. "Resolved" was defined as either fixing the issue with the customer or making sure the query was logged with the right department for resolution. Over 80% of calls were from people questioning the accuracy of their utility bill. Sometimes this could be explained quickly and was accepted, but a lot of the time, the customers were convinced it was wrong. The quickest way to deal with this was to log a request to engineering to send out an engineer to check the meter was working properly. The customer service team was winning accolades across the business for smashing their KPI.

The mapping revealed that less than 2% of the meters checked actually had a technical problem and that over 35% of calls into the customer service team were from customers calling back two or three times or more because they were still waiting for an engineer to come and "fix" their meter.

It was agreed to change the key metric in the customer service call center to "first time resolution"—in other words, the percentage of customers that had their issue fully resolved in the one call and did not need the issue to be logged with another department. This required a training program and coaching of staff and some calls took longer than the target. However, no extra staff were needed as the repeat calls reduced dramatically, no additional engineers were needed, and customers and staff were much happier. One of the regular celebrations introduced was how many customers had thanked the customer service team each day for solving their issue.

TABLE 3.3

Linkage Behaviors

Think Systemically: Linkage	Example Behavior
Leader	Asks questions about the end-to-end processes to ensure people understand the linkages
Manager	Actively promotes and encourages understanding of the end-to-end processes
Associate	Actively seeks to understand how their role contributes to the end-to-end processes

Howard Raiffa, in discussing negotiation, says: "The mediation of internal conflicts can be resolved by linkages with other problems."* However, this is also a good way to consider the principle of Think Systemically. Few business level problems or opportunities are stand-alone, and it is essential to consider the linkages across the whole system before making any changes.

Some examples of the behaviors we would see associated with linkage are shown in Table 3.3.

Some examples of possible Key Behavioral Indicators that could be used for linkage are given below:

- Percentage of employees on short-term temporary placement to a different department to understand the end-to-end process
- Percentage of managers sponsoring improvement projects outside of their own department
- Percentage of employees that have been involved in a cross-functional mapping or problem-solving team in the last six months

SYSTEMS

As the *Shingo Model* demonstrates, systems drive behavior, so it is important to ensure that systems are constantly reviewed and refined to support and encourage the desired behavior. Some examples of the

---

* Raiffa, H. *The Art and Science of Negotiation*. Cambridge, MA: Belknap Press of Harvard University Press, 1982.

high-level systems associated with the principle Think Systemically are improvement management and strategy deployment. Some of the key elements these systems need to include are given below:

- Bottlenecks throughout the enterprise are made visual and clearly defined.
- Work is scheduled with bottlenecks considered.
- Cross-functional team communication is ongoing.
- Training rotations are ongoing between functions.
- Organization is structured around value streams.
- Changes are tested to analyze impact before rolling out.
- There is a structured process for testing changes.
- Everyone has a deep enough knowledge of the value stream to be able to understand processes upstream and downstream.
- There are daily conversations happening around the impact of improvements made and planned.
- Ongoing validation that initiatives are tied to strategic objectives.
- Opportunities are created for everyone to see upstream and downstream.
- There are daily conversations about impact with internal and external customers.
- When changes are being discussed, all those that could be impacted have a voice.

It is useful to reflect on the Improvement Management and Strategy Deployment systems in your own organization and consider how effectively the elements above are embedded in these systems.

A FINAL THOUGHT

Thinking Systemically is not just about the process. Any process to a greater or lesser extent requires people to operate it. Thinking Systemically will only work if we embrace the people and behavioral aspects. It is not enough to try and design the perfect end-to-end process and expect it will operate systemically. Instead, we must also define and work hard at embedding the ideal behaviors that are required that help people to collaborate and build relationships across boundaries. As the psychiatrist Bruce D. Perry says,

> Relationships matter: the currency for systemic change is trust, and trust comes through forming healthy working relationships. People, not programs, change people.*

FURTHER READING

What Does "Systemic" Mean?†

By Marcus Jenal

"We need more systemic approaches!" This claim has gained some traction in the development world. Everybody is talking about how to make development approaches more "systemic." A quick internet research reveals quite a number of results related to development organizations: USAID, USAID, CGAP, GIZ, GIZ, GIZ, and SDC.

The website of SDC's employment and income network, for example, states that: "In order for SDC to increase the outreach and the sustainability of its interventions, E+I promotes a powerful systemic framework for understanding market systems and guiding interventions for more inclusive markets."

But, one might ask, what does "systemic" mean? Is it just a buzzword, or what is hidden behind it? First, we have to differentiate between "systematic" and "systemic," as these two are still often confused. If you do something in a systematic way, you follow a clear methodology in a regular and comprehensive way. Doing something in a systemic way, on the other hand, means that you take the wider system and its behavior into account. While a systematic intervention follows a clear plan in a meticulous and ordered way, a systemic intervention tries to have an impact on the "whole system." This brings us to the discipline of systems thinking or systems theory, which is studying how systems

---

* Perry, B. D. and Szalavitz, M. *The Boy Who Was Raised as a Dog: And Other Stories from a Child Psychiatrist's Notebook—What Traumatized Children Can Teach Us About Loss, Love, and Healing.* New York, NY: Basic Books, 2017.
† Jenal, M. What does "systemic" mean. *Janel.* Available at https://marcusjenal.wordpress.com/2013/02/08/what-does-systemic-actually-mean/#comments

work and how they can be influenced. The following explanation of the concepts around the idea of "systemic" is largely drawn from Bob Williams and Richard Hummelbrunner's book *Systems Concepts in Action: A Practitioner Toolkit*, as I think it gives a very good overview of the topic.

There are various schools of thoughts and applications in systems theory, but there are three ideas that all of them have in common:

- An understanding of interrelationships
- A commitment to multiple perspectives
- An awareness of boundaries

Interrelationships are essentially about how things are connected and with what consequence. There are four important aspects about interrelationships that we need to consider:

1. The dynamic aspects, the way the interrelationships affect behavior of a situation over a period of time
2. The nonlinear aspects, where the scale of "effect" is apparently unrelated to the scale of the cause; often, but not always, caused by feedback
3. The sensitivity of interrelationships to context, where the same intervention in different areas has varying results, making it unreliable to translate a "best" practice from one area to another
4. The massively entangled interrelationships, distinguishing the behavior of "simple," "complicated," and "complex" interrelationships.

Thinking systemically is, however, more than making sense of the way boxes and arrows fit together or how networks operate. Thus, the second concept is about perspectives. Thinking systemically includes how we look at the picture. When people observe the results of interrelationships, they will "see," interpret, and make sense of those interrelationships in different ways. We need to consider two important aspects.

Firstly, the concept of perspectives in thinking systemically pushes us further than just considering stakeholder interests. We need to understand that different stakeholder groups may not share the same perspective, and most importantly, any one stakeholder will hold several different perspectives, not all of which will be compatible with each other. Thinking systemically about perspectives will help us make sense of individual, diverse, and unintended behaviors.

Secondly, perspectives draw the focus away from the perceived "reality" of how the system works and allow us to consider alternatives. We can essentially not only look at the world how it is, but also compare our conclusions with alternative perceptions of what people think the world looks like. Thus, thinking systemically about perspectives gives us a window into motivations through which we can explain and predict unanticipated behaviors.

The third feature of the concept of thinking systemically is based on the realization that we cannot think about everything. Thus, setting *boundaries* around our thinking is not optional. We make situations manageable by setting boundaries. Thinking systemically has to include a process of making this boundary-setting conscious. A boundary determines what is deemed relevant and irrelevant, what is important and what is unimportant, what is worthwhile and what is not, who gets what kind of resources for what purpose and whose interests are marginalized, who benefits and who is disadvantaged. Boundaries are sites where values get played out and disagreements are highlighted. Power issues are often wrapped up in boundaries. Boundaries also determine how we approach a situation, what we expect from it, and what methods we might use to manage it.

So, if we want to call something "systemic," we have to think about whether it covers the three aspects of interrelationships, perspectives, and boundaries to a satisfactory degree, and in an explicit way.

"They" Assessment*

By Bruce Hamilton[†]

Over years of listening to persons describe their work, one single word has surfaced repeatedly as a barometer of what is frequently called "culture." The use of the word *they* in conversation gives me insight into an organization's ability to engage employees and sustain improvement.

---

* Hamilton, B. 2012. Old Lean Dude. Available at: https://oldeleandude.com/2012/02/2/7/they-assessment/

[†] Bruce Hamilton is the president of GBMP, a Shingo Licensed Affiliate. Mr. Hamilton is also a member of the Shingo Academy, and a former member of the Shingo Executive Advisory Board. He led an organization that received Shingo Prize recognition in 1990. He is well-known for his *Toast* kaizen videos, and for the *Old Lean Dude* blog.

The *technical* aspects of Lean I can observe primarily with my eyes:

- The flow of material and information
- The stability, repeatability, and clarity of work
- Adherence to standards
- Alignment of resources to strategic objectives.

These are artifacts, physical manifestations, of Lean and together are necessary to an organization's Lean development. But alone, the technical efforts provide only a cursory understanding of *culture*. For example, too often I visit workplaces that exhibit evidence of Lean tools and systems, but are lacking a *spirit of improvement*. Deming Prize recipient Ryuji Fukuda refers to a "favorable environment" as a work atmosphere that supports employee participation and nourishes that spirit. This environment is not easily visible from the Lean artifacts. In fact, organizations willing and able to spend money can create an appearance of Lean, with no real change in culture at all. One large manufacturer I visited recently actually farms out improvement projects to subcontractors. They are outsourcing Lean implementation—or so they think.

One word gives these companies away: *they*. It's a word that refers variously to management, employees, other departments or divisions, external suppliers, boards of directors—any parties involved in the flow of goods and services to the customer. When I visit a company, I'm not only looking for the use of Lean tools and systems, but I'm also counting *theys*. Let's call it a *They Assessment*.

Sometimes *they* alludes to an adversarial relationship. "*They* don't listen to us," a nurse told me when I asked her about a scheduling snafu that left patients overflowing in a waiting room. "Who are *they*?" I asked. "The docs," she said. "All doctors?" I asked. "Some more than others," she replied. Notice that the pronoun *they* objectifies an entire group.

In other instances, *they* connotes a more passive separation: "*They* won't support these changes" is a concern I hear often, and it could just as well be spoken by top managers or by employees depending on frame of reference. When I'm speaking to a production department, support departments like IT or engineering are often in the *they* category. And the effect is reciprocal. If one function refers to another as *they*, the other department will always respond in kind.

They is a red flag word. Its frequency and location of use in conversation paint a picture of the business environment: favorable or unfavorable.

Organizations with a stronger Lean culture will refer more frequently to "we" in describing their work. In one company, for example, assembly employees repeatedly referred to the engineering department as "we," even though engineering was clearly a separate entity on the organizational chart. The same production department, however, referred to a subassembly department as *they*, even though both departments worked side by side in the same physical area. As organizations develop the favorable environment, *they* is incrementally replaced by "we," the ideal condition being no *theys* at all. Short of that ideal, when I hear the word *they*, I note a relationship problem that is holding back the essential spirit of improvement.

Recently, I visited a company that was considering the Shingo Prize model as a template for company improvement. The plant manager greeted me in the lobby with these words:

"We'd like to know more about the *Shingo Model* and how it can help us improve. We feel like we've made a lot of improvement in the last five years but have hit a plateau."

Indeed, there *were* technical challenges for this company that were apparent on a tour of the shop floor. Operational availability was still low and inventories still too high. But not a single *they* was spoken. In a company of several hundred people, from management to the factory floor, only "we" and "us" were heard. I responded to the plant manager's question,

"The Shingo Prize model will certainly help your plant past its technical plateau, but as far as I can *hear*, your potential for improvement is very high."

How would your plant fare with a *They Assessment*? Which are toughest relationships to forge?

4

Create Constancy of Purpose

Rather than telling people to work better, it is much more productive to set out clear objectives and to provide motivation.

Shigeo Shingo*

This principle focuses on creating unity. An unwavering clarity of why the organization exists, where it is going, and how it will get there enables people to align their actions, as well as to innovate, adapt, and take risks with greater confidence. This principle requires a methodology for communicating company information to every employee, including goals and metrics.

It is about aligning everyone in the organization to a common purpose. The simplest analogy to illustrate this principle is the rowing boat in any race—it goes faster and has a much happier crew if they are all rowing toward the same destination with the same rhythm and a common goal: to get to the finish line as fast as possible and win the race. Chaos ensues if someone decides their rhythm is better or more important than the rest of the team or just decides to do their own thing.

The purpose of the organization needs to be constant over time, constant as it is deployed down through the organization and constant across the functions and departments. In other words, there is a consistent understanding at all levels and in all areas of why the organization exists, what it is trying to achieve, and what the strategic goals are. Walt Disney described the secret of his success as "the four Cs:"

> The four Cs are the secret of my success—curiosity, confidence, courage, and constancy.[†]

---

* Shingo, S. *The Sayings of Shigeo Shingo: Key Strategies for Plant Improvement*. Cambridge, MA: Productivity Press, 1987.

† Generally attributed to Disney, based on the inclusion of the quote in the Disney Employee Handbook first published in 1974.

An excellent summary of why Constancy of Purpose is so critical was given at the 2018. Australian Association of Manufacturing Excellence (AME) conference by President Guy Bulmer* and he has kindly agreed that his introduction to the conference can be reproduced below:

> This year's theme is "Purpose Driven Excellence." When organizations succeed, it's because they know what to do, they understand their mission, and how to achieve it—more importantly, they know why. In order to truly achieve excellence, your company must clearly define the why, as in your purpose for being an organization. It's a strong sense of purpose, and a commitment to achieving that purpose that will help you grow and flourish. All strategies and Lean efforts flow directly from that one crucial element, Purpose. Regardless of the size of your organization, the service you provide, or the products that you make, there is a purpose that drives the company forward.
>
> An organization that embarks upon a journey of purpose-driven excellence recognizes that, in order to succeed, it needs to embody a clear reason to exist beyond just the pursuit of profit. In fact, the companies that work towards the achievement of their purpose have a clear advantage over those that don't. This year's conference is focused on helping you to realize your purpose, and create a lasting impact both within and outside your organization. By starting out with a laser-like focus on your purpose, combined with a commitment to creating a positive culture—one where people can realize their potential, continue to grow, and feel a genuine sense of fulfillment for their contribution to the pursuit of that purpose—will ultimately lead to success on your journey to enterprise excellence.

IS *CREATE CONSTANCY OF PURPOSE* A PRINCIPLE?

In the ENTERPRISE ALIGNMENT workshop, the delegates are asked to explore the principle of Create Constancy of Purpose in order to deepen their understanding. The Shingo Institute uses several criteria to help delegates explore their understanding of this principle in more detail. The

---

* Guy Bulmer is General Manager Tuff Tonneaus and National President Australian Association Of Manufacturing Excellence (AME) . This is an extract from Guy's opening speech to the 2018 AME Australia National conference. Reproduced with permission of Guy Bulmer.

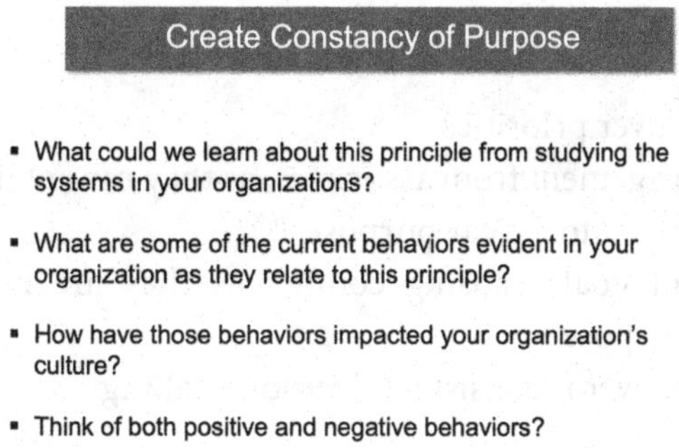

> Create Constancy of Purpose
>
> - What could we learn about this principle from studying the systems in your organizations?
>
> - What are some of the current behaviors evident in your organization as they relate to this principle?
>
> - How have those behaviors impacted your organization's culture?
>
> - Think of both positive and negative behaviors?

FIGURE 4.1
Questions to Create Constancy of Purpose.

reader is encouraged to think about these criteria and consider their own answers. Each of these criteria is explored in more detail below.

IS *CREATE CONSTANCY OF PURPOSE* UNIVERSAL?

Does "Create Constancy of Purpose" apply to everything? Everything has a purpose. This purpose may not be known or understood, but even so, it still exits. Understanding the purpose of anything deepens personal connectivity.

IS IT TIMELESS?

One way to think about this is to ask, "Is there an end point to this principle?" Can you think of any situation where, at some point in time, this principle would cease to apply? A constancy of purpose applies infinitely to everything.

DOES IT HAVE CONSEQUENCES?

Where this principle is not applied, we see time and again a lot of wasted effort and negative impacts.

Negative examples:

- Confusion over priorities
- Lack of engagement from associates, as they cannot understand how they contribute to a clear purpose
- Department goals causing conflict as they are not unified in a common purpose
- Frustration over inconsistent decision-making

Where this principle is applied, we see the opposite of all of the above, but in addition, some of the positive consequences are:

- People have a personal connection with the organization's purpose.
- There is a sense of "one team" across the entire organization.
- Customers get a consistent experience from any interaction with any employee.
- Associates can understand why and how decisions support the organization's purpose.

WHAT HAPPENS WHEN THIS PRINCIPLE IS OBSERVED?

In other words, think about what you would see in organizations where this principle is being applied. For example, it is highly likely that you will be able to observe some of the following:

- People at all levels across the entire organization articulate the purpose with passion.
- People are proud to work for the organization and are advocates for it outside of work.
- People use the purpose as a reference to inform all decision-making.

Shigeo Shingo encourages us to explore the deeper meaning of purpose:

We must learn to think of making progress as moving toward goals, because goals often become means at a higher level. When we think about a goal we are really considering the means toward an even higher-order goal. Thus, it is crucial to understand how goals and means trade places.

For example, to achieve the goal of filling our bellies when we are hungry, we adopt the means of eating. Filling our bellies, however, is only a means for attaining the higher-order goal of taking in nourishment. Similarly, taking in nourishment is actually a means for attaining an even higher-order goal: maintaining life. Etc.

As we can see, goals and means trade places with one another in a chain, and the means or measures we choose will vary considerably depending upon what level of goal we recognize.*

5 WHYS

Applying a 5 Whys analysis can help to deepen our understanding of the principle. See Figure 4.2.

It is useful to try and put this principle into your own context. Ask yourself why this principle is important to your organization. This is a good exercise to deepen understanding of the principle and its application to your organization, and it works well if undertaken by a cross-functional team.

The context, and thus the answers, for each organization will be different, but a generic example is given below.

1. Why is Create Constancy of Purpose of value to our organization?
   Answer: Because we need to unite everyone in the organization in a common purpose we can all believe in.

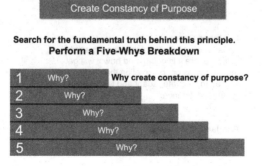

FIGURE 4.2
5 Whys: Create Constancy of Purpose.

---

* Shingo, S. *The Sayings of Shigeo Shingo: Key Strategies for Plant Improvement.* Cambridge, MA: Productivity Press, 1987.

2. Why do we need to do that?

   Answer: Because this will mean that all our systems can be designed and all our decisions informed by this purpose.

3. Why is that important?

   Answer: Because it will mean we can be clear that we are making the right choices and have a shared understanding of why the choices have been made.

4. Why is this important?

   Answer: Because this will ensure we set the right priorities, reduce wasted effort and firefighting, and encourage collaboration.

5. Why is this important?

   Answer: Because it will mean we have a great place to work with highly motivated people that will work together to provide a great service to our customers.

In summary, the Shingo Institute believes that the principle of Create a Constancy of Purpose is important for the reasons outlined in Figure 4.3.

Without this constancy of purpose, any organization becomes a very confusing place to work. Priorities change on a frequent basis, people reactively lurch from one "crisis" to the next, and they quickly lose sight of what it is the organization is trying to achieve. As Benjamin Disraeli, the British Prime Minister and statesman, said: "The secret to success is constancy of purpose."*

Create Constancy of Purpose

Business Case:
An unwavering clarity of why the organization exists, where it is going, and how it will get there enables people to align their actions, as well as to innovate, adapt and take risks with greater confidence.

Fundamental Truth:
Our success depends upon a commitment to a shared understanding of why we exist.

FIGURE 4.3
The importance of Create Constancy of Purpose.

---

* Mr. Disraeli at Sydenham. *The Times*, June 25, 1872.

One organization that continues to drive constancy of purpose in every area of the business is Ozgene Pty Ltd. Still on their Lean journey, Ozgene brings their constancy of purpose to life every day with their customers. One can see it in the day-to-day activities of the business and in their continuous improvement culture, enabling customers to experience it in every engagement.

This short case study, jointly written with Ozgene Chief Executive Officer (CEO) Frank Koentgen, explains the approach taken.

OZGENE CASE STUDY: "TO ADVANCE HUMANITY—INSPIRE CURIOSITY"

It was not that long ago that a mouse was just a mouse. For the team at Ozgene, a mouse represents a way to advance humanity. Ozgene has become a company dedicated to exactly that, and they do it by inspiring curiosity within themselves and their customers.

Today, Ozgene is one of the leading companies providing genetically customized mice for researchers around the world. In fact, 80% of their customers are located outside of Australia. Shipments leave the Ozgene facility almost daily for their destinations in the United States, Europe, Asia, South America, and New Zealand. Ozgene mice can be found in laboratories on almost every continent, from small academic institutions to multinational pharmaceutical companies.

Ozgene's Lean journey started in 2009 when the CEO, Dr. Frank Koentgen, first got hold of the book *The Toyota Way* by Jeff Liker. Intrigued by the book, Frank studied Lean further, including attending the Shingo Study Tour in Japan in May 2012.

At Ozgene, Lean can be best described as "human Lean," centered on the core values of being humble and respectful, as well as building trust and confidence. As part of this, each individual process is humanized, stabilized, standardized, and improved. The implementation of Lean has led to a significant improvement in productivity and a remarkable reduction in project timelines. The Shingo Institute has played a key part in reinforcing and assisting Ozgene's human Lean journey, and Frank has been an executive of the Shingo Executive Advisory Board since 2015.

Frank has sought to embed Ozgene's Constancy of Purpose, "to advance humanity—inspire curiosity," in every aspect of the business, both internally and with customers. Frank explains one element of his approach to help achieve this was to explore some key questions.

The questions we are asking ourselves as a company: Why? How? What? and while the order in which we ask them may change, it is about converting our ideas into solutions to gain a competitive edge. Let's start with why …

Why?

Our why, our raison d'etre, is "to advance humanity." Answering the why leads to alignment. Alignment brings us together as a team—a group of people with a common purpose. People tend to align themselves with why, not with what or how. Both the Ozgene team, as well as our clients, are looking to advance humanity. It is a goal that many of us can identify with.

How?

How do we attempt to achieve our why as well as our business goals? At Ozgene, this is done first and foremost by "inspiring curiosity" in people. This ties in with our vision and our "True North" goals, which are to: 1) develop people, 2) minimize lead time, 3) pursue zero defect, and 4) minimize cost.

Developing people is the key as it allows us to leverage and grow the knowledge in our company. The second goal to minimize lead time facilitates time-based competition, using delivery timelines as a competitive advantage. Pursuing the second goal leads to the third goal: to pursue zero defect, getting the work done right the first time. Zero defect, or the pursuit of it, brings about the fourth goal to minimize cost, aiming to eliminate mistakes and rework.

So how do we actually do this? We separate processes and people, stabilize production over time, harmonize our processes, and thereby visualize deviation and defects. I know this endeavor will never be complete. The more I learn, the more I realize how little I know. There is more frustration on one hand, more opportunity to improve on the other. Always striving for a culture of unattainable organizational excellence.

What?

The what is defined by our clients. It is a privilege to provide products and services that our clients feel add value to them. It does of course mean utilizing and improving our current services and products. And yes, it does also include us exploring new ideas and letting our clients decide whether or not they add value.

			purpose - why?				
to advance humanity							**inspire curiosity**
society	industry	company	system	process	skill	people	

what is curiosity?		
too small => boredom	**just right => curiosity**	too big => anxiety
know ⟵	**GAP** ⟶	*don't know*
1. **un**conscious **in**competence (+/-)	2. conscious **in**competence (-)	(--)
3. conscious competence (+)		
4. **un**conscious competence (++)		
certainty	*uncertainty*	*extreme uncertainty*
	confidence & trust	
	be humble & respectful	

(people grid values: 3, 2 / 4, 1)

FIGURE 4.4
Inspire curiosity.

This approach is summarized in Figure 4.4.

In order to progress from unconscious incompetence to unconscious competence, people need to be inspired with curiosity to start understanding what they do not know. However, this will inevitably lead to uncertainty and potential personal insecurity. As such, leaders are humble and respectful and focus on building mutual confidence and trust through coaching and teaching and learning. At the same time, they ensure that the Constancy of Purpose is clear and consistent, otherwise too much uncertainty will lead to anxiety and confusion.

Let's examine another of the strategic goals, "minimize lead time," in a bit more detail. Lead time is key to Ozgene's customers. Any reduction in lead time means that customers can not only have faster cycles of learning, but also that drugs can be tested sooner and potentially get to market quicker, contributing directly to Ozgene's purpose of advancing humanity.

From 2012 to 2017, average project completion lead times were reduced by 73% or 3.7x fold. In 2017, it was 32 weeks average, and in 2018 it was expected to be 26 weeks average. The target in the near future of 18 weeks is achievable, given that 20 weeks has been achieved already. The relentless encouragement of curiosity—"why can't we do this?"—is key to this achievement, as is the discussion around "how will this help to advance humanity?" In other words, why is it important to achieving the purpose? This discussion and debate is key to people understanding the "why" and being inspired to be curious about how it can be achieved.

On a more mundane level, every day a large number of mouse cages need to be cleaned out. "How does this advance humanity?" is a legitimate question. However, the consequences of not doing this cleaning are clear, and it would have a dramatic impact on the performance of the business, the health of the mice, and the service to the customer. By having an open discussion and talking through just how important this task is, people can see that it is critical to quality and has to be performed to the highest standard every time. It does not mean they necessarily like doing it, but they understand why it has to be done and how to do it at minimum cost with zero defects.

In Ozgene's case, the Constancy of Purpose provides the "why," alignment up, down, and across the whole organization provides the "what and when," and the process provides the "how."

You can learn more about Ozgene and Frank Koentgen's approach to improvement at www.ozgene.com.

CLARITY ON WHAT, WHERE, AND WHY

However, Constancy of Purpose is not as simple as creating a vision or mission statement. These, unfortunately, are often as Dilbert describes them: "Long awkward sentences that illustrate senior leaders' inability to think clearly."*

Instead, Constancy of Purpose comes from being clear on three things:

1. What: This can be a couple of simple sentences about what you are trying to achieve. One of the most effective examples consists of just two words: "Encircle Caterpillar," which was used to focus the Komatsu organization on developing a range of products that beat their main competitor in terms of range and overall customer value. A similar approach is used by Autoliv, whose constancy of purpose is articulated as "We save lives."

---

* Adams, S. *Dogbert's Top Secret Management Handbook*. New York, NY: HarperBusiness, 1996.

2. How: What are the four or five key things you need to do to achieve the "what?" This may be a straightforward bullet list of the key things that need to be delivered. While the "what" statement may last for many years or decades, the "how" statements may well change on a more frequent basis (e.g., annually), or at least the targets associated with them will change.

3. Why: The "what's in it for me" element—a clear and meaningful reason why this is important and why I as an employee should care about it.

It is useful to test any language used with a wide cross-section of the organization. Test out if the intent is understood and change the wording so that it makes sense to everyone, not just the leadership team.

Constancy of Purpose cannot be achieved with one-way communication down through the organization. If the message is just "sent" to people, then at best it will only be partially heard and understood. What is needed is a dialogue that allows open discussion and genuine exploration of the meaning. Providing only written statements or emails will never create a constancy of purpose.

It is possible to test the effectiveness of the communication and deployment of the organization's Constancy of Purpose by asking two simple questions. These questions can be asked by anyone at any level and are especially powerful if asked by leaders across the organization on a regular basis. They are not intended as a test of the person being asked, but rather a test of the effectiveness of the strategy deployment system, how well it has helped people to understand the organization's purpose, and if it has helped achieve a personal connection for associates to the purpose.

Question 1: "How would you describe our organization's purpose?"
If people can answer this question, then the purpose has been well-communicated and people can recite back what they have been told. However, it cannot be said to be effectively deployed unless they can answer a second question.

Question 2: "Can you tell me how you are helping us to deliver our purpose in your role?"
This question is about ensuring people have made the connection between what they do and how it fits with the purpose. Can they relate their day-to-day activity to the purpose? Does it inform and guide their decision-making?

A FILTER

One example is provided by the parent organization of the Shingo Institute, the Jon M. Huntsman School of Business at Utah State University, where since 2006, the purpose has been defined as: "Our purpose is to be a career accelerator for our students and an engine of growth for our community, our state, the nation, and the world."

The purpose statement is extremely useful as a filter and helps keep everyone aligned around a common purpose. For example, there is complete unity among faculty and leadership at the school around the concept that providing students with an education but not being able to place them in a meaningful career is waste. As such, in decision-making discussions, a key question linked to the purpose statement is, "How does this accelerate the careers of our students?" This acts as a very useful filter to help ensure that decisions are aligned to the purpose statement.

DOES CONSTANCY OF PURPOSE MEAN THAT NOTHING WILL CHANGE?

Constancy of Purpose does not mean that nothing will ever change. As Deming said:

> Create constancy of purpose toward improvement of product and service, with the aim to become competitive and to stay in business, and to provide jobs.*

Indeed, some of the most successful organizations in the world combine constancy of purpose with an in-built drive to continuously improve. One such as example is attributed to Roberto Goizueta, Chairman, Director, and Chief Executive Officer of Coca Cola:

> At the end of every day of every year, two things remain unshakable: our constancy of purpose and our continuous discontent with the immediate present.

---

* Deming, W. E. Dr. Deming's 14 Points of Management. The W. Edwards Deming Institute, 2018. Available at https://deming.org/explore/fourteen-points.

Almost every aspect of any organization is always in a constant state of change. Customers change, customers' expectations change, competitors change, markets change, technology changes, leadership and management changes, processes change, products change, strategies change, even values or the implied meaning of those values change. Even knowing this, the first of W. Edwards Deming's "14 Points" is to create constancy of purpose. So, how can this be achieved?

Purpose, at the highest level, answers the question: "Why does this organization exist?" It is incumbent upon leaders to find agreement on philosophical and strategic direction that provides a unifying vision. This sense of direction helps people keep their eyes on the horizon so that when tactical decisions require a temporary detour, they understand why and can contribute to getting back on track. The second category for where constancy of purpose can be achieved is in the establishment of the guiding principles upon which the organization is grounded. Principles are universal, timeless, and self-evident laws that govern the consequences of our actions. The degree to which principles are adhered to will always impact the long-term success of any organization. Leaders must come to understand which principles have the greatest impact on their results and then make certain every aspect of the organization is aligned to drive behavior that is in greatest harmony with the principles.

Having established direction and guiding principles, a leader must align strategy and performance metrics broadly and deeply into the organization. A system must be built to ensure constant communication, both up and down. Changes in direction, guiding principles, and key metrics should be treated like changes in the national constitution. Organizations that frequently redirect philosophies and strategies fail to recognize the tremendous waste associated with instability, fluctuation, and, perhaps most importantly, the loss of human commitment.

This is also recognized and clearly articulated by Jeff Bezos, CEO of Amazon:

> I don't think that you can invent on behalf of customers unless you're willing to think long-term, because a lot of invention doesn't work. If you're going to invent, it means you're going to experiment, and if you're going to experiment, you're going to fail, and if you're going to fail, you have to think long-term.*

---

* Bishop, T. Jeff Bezos explains why Amazon doesn't really care about its competitors. *Geekwire*, 17 September 2013. Available at https://www.geekwire.com/2013/interview-jeff-bezos-explains-amazon-focus-competitors/.

As stated in the introduction, the Shingo Institute believes that "An unwavering clarity of why the organization exists, where it is going, and how it will get there enables people to align their actions, as well as to innovate, adapt, and take risks with greater confidence."

In the video interview shared in the workshop, Brou Gautier, Chief of the USA CPI Division Office of the Deputy Chief Management Officer USAF, describes his understanding of Constancy of Purpose:

> Constancy of Purpose is a key element which makes leaders make sure that their organization can help them achieve their strategic goals because they have the right focus and the right drive to make the improvements required to meet their mission.

Another key element is a focus on the long-term. In his book, *The Toyota Way*, Jeffrey K. Liker highlights the principle of long-term focus, which provides a foundation of stability in the executive suite that can be achieved in no other way. He highlights this as the first of Toyota's 14 principles: "Base your management decisions on a long-term philosophy, even at the expense of short-term financial goals."*

When an organization creates a long-term focus, it is more likely that decisions will pursue safety, quality, delivery, and cost rather than just monthly or quarterly financial targets or bonus cut-offs. In conjunction with taking care of the short- and medium-term priorities, thinking in terms of 20- to 50-year legacy goals significantly reduces the tendencies for knee-jerk reactions to urgent pressures.

ALIGN SYSTEMS AROUND PURPOSE

Another key element is to ensure that systems are aligned to the purpose from the stakeholders' perspective. The full potential is realized only when the most critical aspects of an enterprise share a common platform of principles of operational excellence, management systems, and tools. While it is expected that organizations will develop some unique elements of their local culture, it is also expected that principles become a common, unifying part of each locale. Top-level leadership, staff, and business

---

* Liker, J. *The Toyota Way: 14 Management Principles from the World's Greatest Manufacturer*. New York, NY: McGraw-Hill, 2004.

processes should exemplify the same principles, systems, and tools as the operational components of the enterprise.

It is essential to align behaviors with performance that is focused on driving long-term results. This happens when the systems are aligned with principles of operational excellence. Managers should help each person anchor their own personal values with these same principles. Personal values are what ultimately drive individual behaviors. Leaders are responsible for creating the environment and the process for people to evaluate the correctness of their own values relative to the performance results required of the organization.

For example, one organization the editor visited learned a valuable lesson when they set a business goal to reduce customer complaints, only to find that as they did, they began to lose valuable customers. The measure was driving behavior that made complaining such a painful experience that they just stopped calling. A better measure might have been to increase the number of complaints so that every single disappointment is given an opportunity to be resolved.

THE POLICY DEPLOYMENT SYSTEM

Policy Deployment (also known as Hoshin Kanri) is a planning and implementation system, based on scientific thinking, employee involvement, and respect for the individual. An in-depth explanation of the Hoshin Kanri system is kindly provided by Dr. Rick Edgeman of the Shingo Institute under the "Further Reading" section at the end of this chapter.

At the strategy level, policy deployment provides leadership with the necessary principles, systems, and tools to carefully align key objectives and execution strategies while empowering the organization through cascading levels of detail to achieve those objectives. Because so many people are involved, clarity is critical. An aligned strategy helps keep everyone (literally) on the same (single) page and pointed in the same direction.

One of the key tools to help support strategy deployment is the visual management board (VMB). The VMB is at the heart of the strategy deployment system, providing the focal point for teams to review performance, set priorities, solve problems, and manage continuous improvement activities.

At a high level, the organization should be trying to achieve two things with the VMB:

1. An alignment of the team to True North and customer value, and
2. The team's engagement in wanting to proactively deliver these.

Some key elements that should be included on visual management boards to help achieve this are:

- The VMB must be clearly linked to True North and customer value.
- It must contain measures and targets that demonstrate these links.
- It must contain actions linked to measures.
- It must contain Continuous Improvement (CI) activities linked to True North and customer value.

The VMB, however, has limitations unless it is part of an overall deployment system which includes "huddles" or regular stand-up meetings that take place around the VMB. A VMB is only as good as the quality of the conversation it provokes in these meetings. The times of meetings are planned, fixed to a set timetable, and agreed in a sequence which facilitates cross-learning and enables leaders to be present at more than one meeting during the day. The frequency and timing are determined by the operating rhythm of the team.

The duration of the huddle is fixed and typically takes a maximum of 10–15 minutes. Teams need coaching and guidance on how to make best use of the time and a couple of simple tips can be very useful, for example, the one-minute rule. If a topic is highly relevant to just two people rather than the whole team, then they have a maximum of one minute to discuss it. Any longer than that, the discussion must be taken offline and the answer agreed upon outside of the huddle.

The key is that the focus of the huddle is action-oriented and the team gets value from the discussion. There is a standard agenda and a guide to standard practice for running a huddle. For example, the standard practice could include rotating leadership/facilitation of the huddle among different team members for each meeting. Some elements of a good huddle are that it should be:

- Short and focused
- Review recent performance against targets
- Celebrate successes

- Agree on priorities
- Agree on actions with clear owners and dates and document these on the board
- Be facilitated by different members of the team

STANDARDIZED DAILY MANAGEMENT SYSTEM

Another essential element to achieving constancy of purpose across the organization is Standardized Daily Management. This is the concept of having some level of detailed work description for how to do daily work, applying at all levels of the organization. At a leadership and management level, it is often referred to as "Leader Standard Work." Regardless of the perception among many leaders, their work can and should be organized into standard components. Standard daily management creates a reference point from which continuous improvement can be based. Standard daily management can lead to greater process control, reduction in variability, improved quality and flexibility, stability (i.e., predictable outcomes), visibility of abnormalities, clear expectations, and a platform for individual and organizational learning. Standard daily management enables creativity that is focused and controlled rather than ad hoc. Leaders who follow and insist upon standard work send a clear message that they are serious and no one is above continuous improvement.

One potential example of the application of leader standard work is the system that is put in place around gemba walks. Just one of the advantages that gemba walks provide is the opportunity for leaders to test the effectiveness of the strategy deployment system. They are in no way meant to be used to test or assess the individuals or teams visited but rather to test how well the system has enabled the understanding of the desired knowledge and behaviors. The gemba walks are intended to support, promote, and check. However, they need to be put in place with clear accountabilities around when, who, and how often they should be done. Leaders need to have them fixed in their schedules as part of their daily standard work.

The walks provide the opportunity for meaningful discussions, with the leaders spending far more time actively listening and observing rather than giving advice. An effective gemba walk will leave leaders, managers, and associates feeling valued. For associates and managers, the target condition is that they feel respected as a result of the gemba walk. It should result in a greater sense of ownership and pride in the job they do. For leaders, the gemba walk should give a better understanding of the process and any issues within the process, and should lead to much stronger working relationships.

One organization that has sought to embed a constancy of purpose is Auckland Pools, who are a division of Auckland Council in New Zealand. Their story is shared in the case study below.

AUCKLAND COUNCIL POOLS AND LEISURE CASE STUDY*

Naku te rourou nau te rourou ka ora ai te iwi

(Maori proverb)

My basket and your basket of knowledge, together we grow

(English translation)

Brief Overview of Auckland Council Pools and Leisure

Every great organization has business units, departments, or groups that simply stand out as representing excellence. To achieve excellence, a commitment to continuous improvement must be a way of thinking and behaving across the organization. For Auckland Council, one of the standout entities helping them achieve ongoing business excellence and continuous improvement through their implementation of Base Camp and striving toward Shingo accreditation is their Auckland Council Pools and Leisure Business Unit.

Over the past three years, this business unit and its staff have successfully developed an impressive culture of continuous improvement. This is now future-proofing the performance, integrity, and credibility of this highly successful and continuously evolving Pools and Leisure Operation. The

---

* This case study is an extract from a forthcoming book planned for publication in 2020: *Lean Leisure—Striving for Enterprise Excellence in Auckland Pools and Leisure* by Chris Butterworth, Louis Sylvester, and Richard Steel.

team is constantly exploring, reviewing, re-inventing, and striving for continuous improvement across all of its operations, resulting in a business unit with superior staff performance and highly respected services that meet the needs of the local community, its user groups, visitors, and customers.

Auckland Council Pools and Leisure recognized that there was an essential ingredient required if long-term success and sustainability were to be achieved to better service the needs of the Auckland Community. With the global recession over recent years, it was evident that times were becoming increasingly tighter for residents and ratepayers alike. Ratepayers simply could not continue to endure unaffordable rate increases year after year. Auckland Council recognized this and was responsive to these issues by exploring what opportunities were available to best assist in providing better local services for less.

What Is the Purpose?

The purpose of Pools and Leisure is to directly contribute and align to the organization's overarching vision of "creating the world's most livable city." In order to deliver on this purpose, it was evident that the Pools and Leisure business unit needed to clearly understand the actual Plan for Aucklanders both now and into the future. At a very high level, the plan, both now and in the long-term, translated as follows.

A Plan for All Aucklanders / TE MAHERE A TĀMAKI MAKAURAU – MĀ TE KATOA O TĀMAKI MAKAURAU

The Auckland Plan is the strategy to make Auckland an even better place than it is now and create the world's most livable city (Figure 4.5). It shows how it will prepare for the additional one million people they may have to accommodate by 2040, and the 400,000 new homes needed. Many people were involved in the preparation of this plan: Auckland residents, community groups, infrastructure providers, central government, iwi (indigenous tribes), business groups, and voluntary organizations who helped shape the plan for Auckland's future. Although the mayor and Auckland Council led its development, the Auckland Plan is for all of Auckland and all Aucklanders, and its successful implementation will require leadership, action, investment, and commitment from many organizations, groups, and individuals.

FIGURE 4.5
Auckland Mission.

Auckland Now and Into The Future / TE TŪMANAKO MĀ TĀMAKI
MAKAURAU

Auckland's vision is to become the world's most livable city. As the world's most livable city, Auckland will be a place that:

- Aucklanders are proud of,
- They want to stay or return to, and
- Others want to visit, move to, or invest in.

The goal of livability expresses the shared desire to create a city where all people can enjoy a high quality of life and improved standards of living, a city which is attractive to mobile people, firms, and investors, and a place where environmental and social standards are respected (see Table 4.1).

The Long-Term Plan 2012–2022

The Long-Term Plan (LTP) sets out the council's projects and budget for the next ten years. It is the starting point for turning the aspirations of the Auckland Plan into an implementation plan. This aligns with the mayor's vision to create the world's most livable city.

How Do You Align to the Purpose?

Auckland Council Pools and Leisure aligned to the purpose of "creating the world's most livable city" through the development of a Game Plan. This tailored Game Plan was a three-year transformational program

Create Constancy of Purpose • 77

TABLE 4.1

Auckland Vision

Auckland's Vision

The World's Most Livable City

Outcomes: What the Vision Means in 2040

| A fair, safe and healthy Auckland | A green Auckland | An Auckland of prosperity and opportunity | A well connected and accessible Auckland | A beautiful Auckland that is loved by its people | A culturally rich and creative Auckland | A Maori identity that is Auckland's point of difference in the world |

designed to directly align with and deliver on Auckland Council's vision through achieving the goals of Pools and Leisure, those goals being:

- Inspiring more Aucklanders to be active
- Inspiring children, young people, and whānau (family) to reach their potential
- Delivering an operationally cost-neutral network

By "more Aucklanders," the Pools and Leisure business unit meant specifically those who recognized the benefit of being active, but face a myriad of opportunity and confidence challenges that make them "insufficiently active." In short, Pools and Leisure wanted to grow the market, not their market share, thus inspiring more Aucklanders to be active.

The Game Plan was built around the premise that if Pools and Leisure target the right people, and create and demonstrate value for the customers, then their business would grow and they would become less dependent on ratepayers. This meant being driven by the customer needs, looking to continuously improve, and using their size and scale to their advantage so that they could deliver better value for Aucklanders.

What Is the Game Plan?

In order to align the entire organization, the strategy was deployed deliberately using words that people would connect with in their work environment. Hence "The Game Plan" sought to describe on a page what the organization was trying to achieve—in other words, "how to win the game" (Figure 4.6). The customers were described as "fans" and the employees as "players in the team." A "playbook" helped people understand what role or "position" they needed to play in the game and a detailed player "profile" described expectations and requirements for each role. This process helped to bring the strategy to life, as people understood what they needed to do to make a difference and help achieve the strategic goals.

Continuous improvement supports all elements of the Game Plan, in part by reducing waste to create more time and increase creativity and innovation for all Auckland Pools and Leisure employees. This is centered on the heart of continuous improvement, being the unswerving pursuit of operational excellence, and in seeking and delivering true value to their customers, or "fans," in everything that they do.

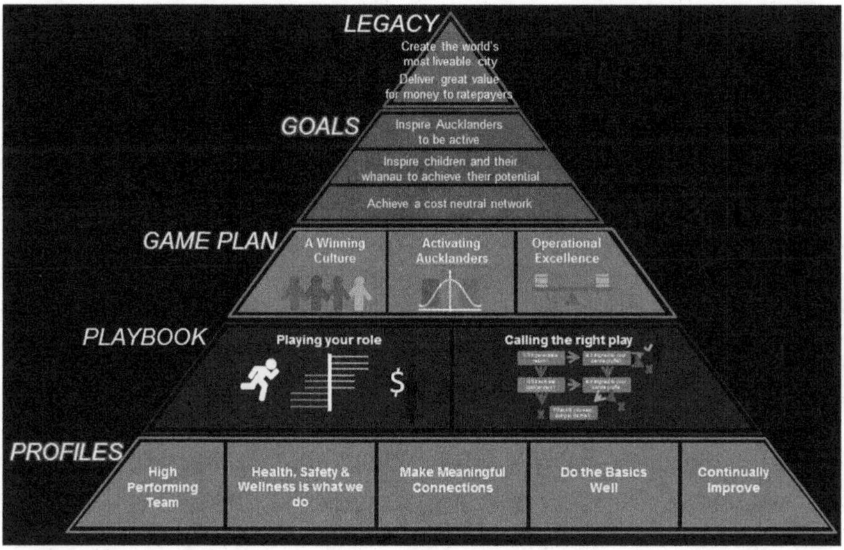

FIGURE 4.6
Game Plan.

Auckland Pools and Leisure is one of the early adopters in New Zealand to have demonstrated a leading position of how CI can be applied within the local government sector. Their strategy deployment process aligns the strategic goals of the organization with a cascade of increasingly specific programs and activities that support these goals. This deployment shows the long-term focus (the next ten years), goals, and objectives, and then focuses on what needs to be accomplished in the following year. Each department has been able to align their annual goals to this strategic plan focus, coupled with improvement priorities and measuring outcomes through key performance indicators.

This means staff are working toward the goal of providing perfect value to the customer through a perfect value creation process that has zero waste. The Pools and Leisure centers are not only meeting today's deliverables, but have strategically positioned themselves to continuously improve and evolve to address the challenges of tomorrow and beyond.

BEHAVIORAL BENCHMARKS

The Shingo Institute believes that the understanding of the principle Create Constancy of Purpose can be deepened by considering what are referred to as "behavioral benchmarks." These are intended to help us look at the principle from many different perspectives and act as a guide or reference point to help define behaviors that support this principle. It is not the intention that the application of this principle is limited to only these behavioral benchmarks, as it is important to remember that the context of every organization is unique. However, they provide a very useful basis for further discussion and exploration of the principle. The behavioral benchmarks for Create Constancy of Purpose are Alignment, Clarity, and Communication. These are explored in more detail below.

Alignment: Our common sense of purpose drives all our decisions.

Dictionary definition: Arrangement in a straight line or in correct relative positions.

One of the classic phrases that is used to illustrate alignment is "We are all singing off the same hymn sheet." The music analogy works well as, with alignment, the people in an organization will all be in harmony with the purpose.

A famous story that helps illustrate alignment is the story of Kennedy's visit to the NASA space center in the early 1960s. When President Kennedy saw the janitor carrying a broom and asked him what he was doing, the janitor's reply was: "I'm helping put a man on the moon."[*]

This associate understood that if the toilets were not kept clean and this led to one of the astronauts becoming sick, then the mission could be put in jeopardy. He was clear on the purpose of the organization and on what his role was in helping to achieve it.

Another similar example is given in a story about Christopher Wren, a famous architect who designed some of the most magnificent buildings in the UK, including St. Paul's Cathedral. The story goes that Wren was a regular visitor to the building site and engaged in conversations with the workmen. One day, he stopped several workmen and asked them, "What are you doing?"

The first response he got was, "I am cutting this stone."

The response from the second workman was, "I am earning five shillings two pence a day."

But the response from the third workman was, "I am helping Sir Christopher Wren build a beautiful cathedral."

---

[*] Nemo, J. What a NASA janitor can teach us about living a bigger life. *The Business Journals*, December 23, 2014. Available at https://www.bizjournals.com/bizjournals/how-to/growth-strate gies/2014/12/what-a-nasa-janitor-can-teach-us.html.

TABLE 4.2

Alignment Behaviors

Create Constancy of Purpose: Alignment	Example Behavior
Leader	Continuously communicates the common purpose of the organization
Manager	Builds regular discussion of the common purpose into daily activities
Associate	Asks questions and shares experiences that help embed understanding of how they contribute to the common purpose

The first workman knew his job, the second knew he received a wage to complete tasks, but the third understood how he contributed to the greater purpose.* This story is unverified but nevertheless is a very good illustration of alignment.

Some examples of behaviors that support the behavioral benchmark of alignment are given in Table 4.2.

Some potential KBIs for Alignment are given below:

- Percentage of employees that can explain how they personally contribute to the purpose
- Percentage of improvement suggestions that explicitly reference the purpose
- An employee feedback rating on "catchball" discussions

Clarity: Our contribution to society is so clear to everyone that it unifies our organization.

Dictionary definition: The quality of being clear; the quality of being coherent and intelligible.

With clarity, we are seeking to ensure that the message is clear, precise, and meaningful. The shorter and the more straightforward the language, the better. As Schumacher said:

Any intelligent fool can make things bigger and more complex. It takes a touch of genius and a lot of courage to move in the opposite direction.†

---

* Platt, S. *Respectfully Quoted: A Dictionary of Quotations Requested from the Congressional Research Service.* Washington, D.C.: Library of Congress, 1989.
† Schumacher, E. F. Work in a Sane Society. *Schumacher Center*, January 1972. Available at https://centerforneweconomics.org/publications/work-in-a-sane-society/.

Too often, there is a lot of confusion around vision and mission statements, and organizations send out conflicting and sometimes bewildering messages, leaving employees wondering what it all means. Each one might make sense in isolation, but often there are too many and the clarity is lost. On one recent site visit, the editor was shown the company vision and mission statement clearly displayed on the wall. He was then shown the thirty-page strategy document, which looked very professional, but intriguingly did not contain the vision and mission statements. Then he was shown the detailed departmental strategy document, which must have taken many hours to produce. It looked amazing. It was, however, difficult to spot how it related to the company strategy document. He was assured that it did, but people struggled to explain how. He went on to find out that every department had produced their own strategy document and that they had not consulted, let alone collaborated, on the content. It quickly became apparent that, for many people, it was a very confusing place to work.

Too often the clarity is in the heads of a few senior people, but it gets lost as it is deployed down the organization. Many years ago, the editor was talking to one of his colleagues in an organization he had recently joined. Here is a summary of the conversation:

Colleague: "I've been asked to write up a new three-year rolling strategy plan for my department."

Editor: "That sounds interesting. I've never done one of those before."

Colleague: "Well, you will probably get asked for one, as we have to do them every year, but don't worry about it. It's pretty straightforward."

Editor: "Really? Sounds like a lot of work. Don't you need to read the group strategy and link everything into that?"

Colleague: "You've got to be joking. Have you seen the group strategy? You'd need a degree in nuclear physics to decipher that. No, the easiest thing to do is just change the date at the top of the one that was done last year and then add 5% on all the figures two years from now and 10% onto all the figures for three years from now."

Editor: "Is that what you did last time?"

Colleague: "Yes. This will be my fourth one and no one's ever queried it. I think they just tick a box at group HQ to say it's done. I'm convinced no one actually reads it."

Even today when the editor tells this story at conferences, there are always several people in the audience nodding in recognition of a similar experience.

One of the video speakers in the ENTERPRISE ALIGNMENT & RESULTS course is Dan Bowes, who at the time was the general manager of the team at the Commonwealth Bank of Australia that received a Shingo Silver Medallion in 2015. Dan shares his view on the Principle of Constancy of Purpose:

> Constancy of Purpose is really important. It's important that people know why they are at work. It's important people know what things are most important and what they need to focus on, and it's important to have something that binds the whole team together. So, for us, this is our group vision, which is "excelling at securing and enhancing the financial wellbeing of people, business, and communities." So, having that in mind and having it at the heart of all your decision-making means that people are making decisions for the right reasons. What you see are people making that decision consciously with that True North in mind. Customer outcomes are improved by the alignment of people's activities with the organization's purpose.

Dan also wrote a case study to share his experience, and an extract from this is reproduced below, with permission of the authors, from a longer case study published in the book *4+1: Embedding a Culture of Continuous Improvement in Financial Services** by Morgan Jones, Chris Butterworth, and Brent Harder.

COMMONWEALTH BANK OF AUSTRALIA CASE STUDY: EMBEDDING A CONSTANCY OF PURPOSE

This case study of a major Australian bank covers a large-scale operation focused on working with retail banking customers. In order for the team to be successful, there was a need to develop a Constancy of Purpose around delivering customer-focused solutions and interactions. The Constancy of Purpose that was embedded across the business unit was "to enhance the financial well-being of our customers." As one of the key responsibilities of this unit was debt recovery, this constituted a major challenge to traditional thinking.

The business unit had many sub-teams, multiple internal and external stakeholders, and a patchy history of success or failure. By focusing on this Constancy of Purpose, the business unit became one team and ended

---

* Butterworth, C., Harder, B. and Jones, M. *4+1: Embedding a Culture of Continuous Improvement in Financial Services.* Cartridge Family, 2017.

up gaining recognition internally (company's annual productivity and leadership awards) and externally (Shingo Silver Medallion, PEX Award for Culture) for their continuous improvement performance. Examples of achievements included:

- Delivering year on year cost productivity of 10% or more
- Shifting under-performing employee cultures to global best-in-class (independently benchmarked)
- Improving business outcomes including customer quality by 15% annually
- Fostering a watertight operational risk management environment

The business leaders had to decide how to embed this new Constancy of Purpose in a business where the business itself is highly complex, operates in a very sensitive environment, and experiences the typically high staff turnover of any service operations unit.

An additional constraint common to financial services businesses is the high cost of large-scale systems changes and the historical experience of planned deliverables not matching actual outcomes.

While the very top leaders (general manager and senior executives) were brought into these teams from outside the organization, the remaining executive and senior management teams either remained in place or were filled with existing company employees. These new top leaders were experienced Lean practitioners. At the start, there was some existing awareness of continuous improvement, but little practice.

The leadership team therefore focused on two interrelated questions:

1. How do we develop a system that changes the way the existing leaders think and also produces sufficient new leaders of the right caliber on an ongoing basis?
2. How do we build a self-sustaining culture which meets the holistic business challenges coming up and delivers the Purpose?

Of initial critical importance was crystallizing what success looked like and turning that into a compelling vision of the future that everyone (approximately 850 employees in one instance) could understand and get behind. The leaders judged that this would engender the right conditions for a desired optimistic approach to change and start to inspire all employees to want to be a part of the journey.

While acknowledging the continuous nature of ongoing improvement, the leadership team started by using Lean thinking to set a series of time-bound process change goals. Two examples were improving the design and use of technology and resource planning to ensure customer contact occurred only when most convenient for customers, and removing bottlenecks from lengthy legal processes to provide certainty to customers faster than ever before. It is key to the success of the business units in this case study that functional expertise was combined with solid Lean expertise to conceptualize what "good" looked like from the customer and business perspective and to deliver financial benefits early on.

The next step was to blend these "hard" changes with an overall sense of purpose aligned with the higher-level company's vision and strategy around customer-centricity. First, each team of roughly 15 people was tasked with creating a Customer Value Proposition, taking a lead from the company's vision, which could then be synthesized into a True North for the whole business unit. Facilitated sessions then helped the teams "backwards image" into the future to describe what the customer experience would be like and what the business unit would look like in a few years' time. From there, the team developed a set of strategic pillars, such as only investing in technology where it supported the True North, or focusing on developing a broader range of solutions for customers. A multi-modal communications effort was then devised and rolled out (through workshops, town halls, intranet, huddles, etc.) to deliver the coherent plan, seek further input, and motivate people to commit themselves to the plan.

The True North and the pillars became a shorthand used by staff within the business as a mirror/sense-check for activities as diverse as holding conversations with customers on the phone to prioritizing projects. Similarly, the balance achieved between customer outcomes, shareholder outcomes, and community (stakeholder/regulator) outcomes was vital in creating strategic alignment with upstream business units. It created a common bond, too, describing shared expected customer-centric behaviors and building informal relationships between staff members.

"CATCHBALLING"

One of the approaches that helps to achieve clarity is often referred to as "catchball."

Quite simply, if someone throws you a ball, you catch it and throw it back. The idea is that strategic objectives linked to the purpose are "caught," examined, and thrown back and forth for discussion, understanding, and refinement. In effect, it is a key tool in the Check of a good Plan, Do, Check, Act deployment process.

It is the process of encouraging and enabling two-way discussion about the goals and objectives that are being deployed. Leaders and managers need to invest time in making sure that the right conversations take place and people can ask questions to deepen their understanding. Working well, it can also lead to the refinement of targets. For example, if a target has been divided among several teams or departments, but the catchball process reveals that, while for genuine reasons, one department is going to struggle with their target, another area is able to make up the shortfall so that the total goal is still achieved. The original targets can then be adjusted accordingly.

EXAMPLES OF IDEAL BEHAVIORS

Some example of behaviors that support the behavioral benchmark of clarity are given in Table 4.3.

Some potential Key Behavioral Indicators for "clarity" are given below:

- Percentage of employees that can score more than 95% on an anonymous and fun quiz about what the purpose means
- Percentage of employees that have confirmed they have taken part in a "catchball" discussion that helped them understand the purpose
- An employee feedback rating on how deeply they understand and believe in the purpose

TABLE 4.3

Clarity Behaviors

Create Constancy of Purpose: Clarity	Example Behavior
Leader	Ensures language used is clear and simple in all communications
Manager	Encourages two-way discussion to deepen understanding and welcomes questions from associates
Associate	Asks regular questions to ensure full understanding of the goals and objectives

Communication: Everyone knows who we are and why we exist and this is manifested in our daily actions and communications among ourselves and with others.

Dictionary definition: The imparting or exchanging of information by speaking, writing, or using some other medium.

Too often we hear people in organizations say things like, "I don't know about the strategy, that's the big boss's job." Too often the response to this from senior leaders is, "Of course they know the strategy, I've told them what it is at least twenty times. How often do I need to tell them?"

To quote William H. Whyte:

> The biggest problem in communication is the illusion that it has taken place.*

The key to communication is to accept that it is the responsibility of the sender to ensure that people have understood the message. If they don't, then it is not the fault of the person receiving the communications; rather this tells the sender that they need to communicate with more clarity and most likely in a number of different ways.

A useful methodology to apply to communication is Plan, Do, Check, Act.

Plan: What is the key message we want to get across?

Do: Communicate it in a number of ways.

Check: Talk to people to find out if the message has been understood correctly.

Act: If understood, then seek to understand what it was that made it effective. If not understood, then go back to Plan and start again.

Very rarely is the "check" carried out. But if it is not, how do we know if our communication has been effective?

When Marcel Schabos, retired CEO who led the transformation of several global organizations, including Cogent, was asked what his top three lessons were in a successful business transformation, his reply was:

> Number 1: Communication. Number 2: Communication. Number 3: Communication. You can never over-communicate.†

---

* Whyte, W. H. Is Anybody Listening? *Fortune*, September 1950.

† Schabos, M. Interview by Peter Hines. In *Staying Lean*. Hines, P. Lean Enterprise Research Centre: Wales, UK, 2008.

As James Humes, the author and former presidential speechwriter, says:

The art of communication is the language of leadership.*

One story that illustrates how easy it is to get the communications wrong was witnessed by the editor a few years ago. While carrying out a supplier assessment, he observed an associate in the dispatch bay putting white dots onto a complex subassembly before they were subsequently loaded for shipping. The associate would pick up the subassembly, put it into a pre-set jig and then put white dots of correction fluid in several places. He then put the subassembly back into the pallet rack and took out the next one. Intrigued, the editor spoke to him.

Editor: "Excuse me, I notice you are very busy, but I just wondered if you can explain what you are doing?"

Associate: "Well, I'm putting white dots on these subassemblies before they go to the customer."

Editor: "I see. It looks like you are fairly fast at it."

Associate: "Well yes, I've been doing it for a few days now. We have to do it for every one of these before it goes out. I've got a rhythm now and it's really efficient. I'm much faster than the guy who was doing it before."

Editor: "That's great. Tell me, why are you putting the dots on?"

Associate: "It's a customer requirement. I've been told nothing can get on a truck to ship unless it has these dots on it."

Editor: "Do you know why that is?"

Associate: "It's just what the customer insists on. We've got to keep them happy, you know. If they want white dots, then that's up to them."

Editor: "Thanks very much for your time."

The editor then sought out the operations director.

Editor: "I noticed you have a guy in the dispatch bay putting white dots on every one of the main subassemblies you make."

Operations Director: "Yes. Is there a problem?"

---

* Humes, J. The Art of Communication is the Language of Leadership. *International Trade.* March 27, 2008. Available at http://www.freshbusinessthinking.com/the-art-of-communication-is-the-language-of-leadership/.

Editor: "No, I just wondered why it was necessary."

Operations Director: "We had a few quality issues some time back and our commitment to the customer is that we now do 100% visual inspection on the Critical to Quality points. The white dots confirm we have checked them to the required standard before they are shipped. We agreed with the customer that this was a good mistake-proofing system to ensure we didn't miss any of the points."

Editor: "Um. I think something may have gone wrong with the communication system somewhere."

The associate was doing his best to do a good job. He had even found a way to do to it more efficiently and was proud of this. Unfortunately, the communication about why it was important had been totally missed. This was not his fault.

Some example of behaviors that support the behavioral benchmark of communication are given in Table 4.4.

Some potential KBIs for communication are given below:

- Rating system on percentage of employees that are passionate about the purpose
- Percentage of employees on random checks that can explain the purpose
- An employee feedback rating on how effective communications are about the purpose

TABLE 4.4

Communication Behaviors

Create Constancy of Purpose: Communication	Example Behavior
Leader	Frequently communicates a clear, consistent purpose
Manager	Checks that the purpose is understood and deployed to all team members through regular referral to the purpose in decision-making
Associate	Asks questions to deepen knowledge and understanding of the purpose and how it applies in their role

SYSTEMS

As the *Shingo Model* demonstrates, systems drive behavior, so it is important to ensure that systems are constantly reviewed and refined to support and encourage the desired behavior. Some examples of the high-level systems associated with the principle Create a Constancy of Purpose are the Strategy Deployment and Communication systems. Some of the key elements these systems need to include are given below:

- Purpose is always a consideration in decision-making.
- Everyone sees where they fit in the vision.
- There are daily reminders of mission and vision.
- Goals are visual and understood; everyone knows if they are winning or losing.
- There is a structured process used to align goals and strategic priorities that are simple and visible throughout the organization.
- Leaders hold to principles even during rough times.
- Business decisions are made with purpose considered.
- Decisions are made based on long-term thinking.
- People relate to a vision that creates a sense of urgency, unity, and loyalty.
- Everyone describes what they do in terms of purpose.
- Social improvement activities are commonplace.
- Organizational performance is shared openly and regularly.
- Managers coach associates to help prioritize activities to organizational objectives.
- Leaders and managers have standard work that enables them to monitor and maintain alignment.
- There is ongoing, well-defined coaching and training.
- Visits by leaders and managers to the place where work happens are frequent.
- Information systems provide direct flow of important information that can be easily accessed.
- There is a defined structure in place to communicate with everyone daily.

It is useful to reflect on the Strategy Deployment and Communication systems in your own organization and consider how effectively the elements above are embedded in these systems.

FURTHER READING

Hoshin Kanri: Translating "Big Vision" from Strategy to Execution*

By Rick Edgeman[†]

Part 1: Hoshin Kanri—Concept Origins

Prior to World War II, the U.S. share of the world export market was approximately 30%. In the aftermath of World War II, that share grew to more than 70%—a result of a generally healthy and educated workforce, as well as a U.S. infrastructure that remained largely untouched by the war. In contrast, many European and Asian nations were left to deal with infrastructure devastation and human tragedy alike, often with less educated workforces using antiquated equipment.

Given that context, American manufacturers were generally able to sell all that they were able to manufacture, whether what that produced was of superior, average, or inferior quality. It is simple, but inaccurate to assume—especially when basking in the afterglow of World War II victory—that American superiority was responsible for this growth in market share and consequent relative prosperity.

Relatively unnoticed was the role played by instruction in and active spread of quality control methods in American industry during World War II by such luminaries as W. Edwards Deming and Joseph M. Juran, as well as other, usually uncredited, individuals. Those methods proved fundamental to, for example, production of superior quality military equipment, such as tanks. This is not, of course, intended to imply that quality control methods were solely responsible for the Allied victory in World War II, but only that these were an important factor.

After World War II, many of those Americans trained in quality control methods (women) left the workforce and returned to the home.

---

* Available at: https://blog.shingo.org/2016/03/hoshin-kanri-translating-big-vision-from-strategy-to-execution

[†] Rick Edgeman is the Shingo Institute's research director and clinical professor of management in the management department of the Jon M. Huntsman School of Business at Utah State University. He is also appointed to the Quality Science Division of Sweden's Uppsala University and Interdisciplinary Center for Organizational Architecture at Denmark's Aarhus University. Dr. Edgeman has authored more than 200 publications on quality management, sustainability, leadership, innovation, and statistics.

Over the next decades, many of the lessons learned were lost. This was one of at least two things happening concurrently, with the other being that the same "quality gurus" largely responsible for teaching quality methods to approximately 30,000 members of America's World War II workforce began, out of empathy for the plight of the Japanese people, to teach those same methods in Japan, with the belief that those methods could significantly aid the long climb Japan would need to make from the devastation of World War II.

What Deming, Juran, and others found in Japan was a highly talented, highly motivated collection of business and engineering leaders who embraced these methods with near "tent revival" zeal, and who not only widely and expertly adapted and deployed these methods, but who added new and highly pragmatic approaches. This was done with the sort of efficiency that extreme resource scarcity can motivate, augmented by the effectiveness that dedication to precision births. Just as Deming, Juran, Armand Feigenbaum, Philip Crosby, H. James Harrington, Walter Shewhart, and other American quality luminaries wielded significant influence, a new constellation of Japanese "quality stars" arose, the names and developments of whom have been and remain integral to contemporary expressions of quality in its many forms that include, but are not limited to, Lean enterprise methods and Six Sigma—individuals such as Shigeo Shingo and single-minute exchange of die (SMED or quick changeover); Taiichi Ohno and the Toyota Production System (TPS) that resides at the heart of the Lean manufacturing movement; Masaaki Imai and kaizen (continuous improvement); Kauro Ishikawa and cause-and-effect diagrams; Yoji Akao and quality function deployment; Genichi Taguchi and robust product design; Noriaki Kano and the customer needs model; and hoshin kanri—the development of which is not attributed to any single individual, but rather the first use of the term appears to have originated at Japan's Bridgestone Tire company in 1965 (Watson, 2003).

This combination of zeal, expertise, methodological innovation and application, and relentless pursuit of perfection began to have an effect on the American share of the world export market—one that was scarcely noticed until American manufacturers surrendered consumer electronics and automotive markets to Japanese manufacturers—victims not only of Japanese drive and ingenuity, but of their own arrogance and a sense that it was "impossible" for anyone else to out-perform, out-create, or out-innovate American enterprises. The result of this was that, by 1990, the U.S. share of the world export market had fallen to its pre-World War II level of about 30%. Today that share ranges between 10% and 15%, and the U.S. has become the world's greatest debtor nation.

Much has been and continues to be written about the "Japanese miracle," though some of the sheen has dimmed as Japan's economy, like many others, has struggled in recent years. Still, books such as *World Class Manufacturing* by Schonberger (1986), *Kaizen* by Imai (1986), *The Machine that Changed the World* by Jones, Womack, and Roos (1990), and numerous others have had significant impact on the way many global enterprises do business. This is especially so in select sectors such as the automotive industry that have embraced Lean philosophies and methodologies. Increasingly, this is also seen in such sectors as healthcare and banking.

While each of the strategies and methods cited provide value to enterprises using them, we will focus primarily on hoshin kanri, which is essentially an organizing framework that directs enterprise-wide attention to corporate purpose, aligns priorities with local plans, integrates these into daily management and activities, and facilitates enterprise learning and enculturation through routine review (Witcher and Butterworth, 2000).

Part 2: Hoshin Kanri—A Valuable Concept

Roots of *Hoshin Kanri* may be traced to, at least, *A Book of Five Rings* written in 1645 by Miyamoto Musashi (Harris, 1982). This book, the essence of which is captured by the word *heiho* or *strategy*, was a resource intended to provide instruction to samurai warriors, including instruction in what is perhaps the quintessential samurai skill: *kendo*, or precision swordsmanship. Relative to *kendo*, *A Book of Five Rings* asserts that those thoroughly conversant with strategy will recognize the intentions of their enemies and through preparation and recognition will have many opportunities to cultivate and execute strategies capable of thwarting the objectives of their adversaries and positioning themselves to be victorious.

Like *heiho*, the word *hoshin* is comprised of two Chinese characters: *ho*, which means method or form, and *shin*, which is often translated as "shiny metal–the glint from the spear that leads the way" (Lee and Dale, 1998) or, in a more contemporary form, an aim. When assembled, the word *hoshin* can be taken to mean "a methodology for strategic direction setting." The word *kanri* is commonly interpreted as "management" so that *hoshin kanri* becomes "management of the strategic direction setting process." Given this interpretation, in the West, *hoshin kanri* is commonly referred to as either *policy deployment* or *strategy deployment* or often by the East/West hybrid term that we will henceforth use: *hoshin planning*.

Generally speaking, a given *hoshin* is mission and vision critical to an enterprise and is stated in terms of a goal or objective—that is, a policy or a strategy—that is intended to elevate associated business processes and outcomes to a target performance level. The underlying structure of *hoshin* planning implies that it can be applied at essentially any level of the enterprise, ranging from senior executive level to the day-to-day operational level.

Often, a high level (senior executive) *hoshin* is of such foundational importance to the enterprise that failure to attain or fulfill it within an appropriate timeframe will place the organization at risk. As such, a high level *hoshin* can be thought of as representing "big (enterprise) vision." Organizations that practice enterprise level *hoshin* planning ordinarily have a limited number of *hoshin*, typically three to five, that must be realized within a specified time span that, in the West, will ordinarily range from one to five years, with specified mileposts and periodic stage gate reviews along the way.

Those of us in the northern hemisphere can relate to a *hoshin* as an organizational north star or True North, whereas those of us in the southern hemisphere may think of a *hoshin* in relation to the Southern Cross: *hoshin* are intended to aid enterprise navigation and alignment by riveting collective enterprise focus on their attainment.

At the enterprise level, *hoshin* planning begins with "big vision" that is progressively unfolded by cascading the various *hoshin* from one level of the enterprise to the next to the next and so on, beginning with the executive level and ending with the operational level. Thus, from one level to the next to the next until the bottom of the waterfall, an increasingly detailed scheme emerges. In this way, *hoshin* planning begins with strategy or policy, is progressively transformed into a plan that is progressively executed, leading to full strategy/policy implementation. *Hoshin* planning beginning at the operations level is executed in like manner, but with generally less far-reaching strategic implications and nearer-term fulfillment needs. In its high-level incarnation, *hoshin* planning is highly strategic and focused on breakthrough improvement (Witcher, 2003), whereas at the operations level, it is ordinarily on more incremental, continuous improvement (Hutchins, 2008).

We can conclude that a key benefit of *hoshin* planning is its ability to create consensus (Watson, 2003) and facilitate enterprise alignment through significant workforce participation (Kondo, 1998) that requires extensive communication that is both lateral and multi-level in nature. Such communication assures that each individual involved in the *hoshin* planning process is conversant with the "big goals and objectives" or *hoshin* of those both immediately before them (their direct supervisor) and immediately following them (their direct reports) as well, usually, with those of their immediate colleagues. This occurs because their own *hoshin* and related activities are driven by *hoshin* received from their direct supervisor and in turn inform the *hoshin* and related activities of their direct reports so that all involved in the process are familiar with three or more levels. This communication process is fundamentally a negotiated dialogue that is often referred to as "catchball" (Tennant and Roberts, 2001) and "connects the planners and the doers" (Sussland, 2002). Successful *hoshin planning* implementation is often associated with complementary and skilled use of effective performance management and measurement approaches such as the balanced scorecard (Kaplan and Norton, 1996; Witcher and Chau, 2007). Together these approaches provide an exceptional means of rationally applying management of objectives as developed by the father of modern strategic management: Peter Drucker (Greenwood, 1981).

The value of *hoshin* planning, as with most approaches, is bounded by the value and timeliness of the strategy or policy being deployed, not to mention the quality of the "plan" as it unfolds through the organization. Figure 4.7 provides a view of the larger context within which *hoshin* planning typically occurs. Although *hoshin* planning may begin at any level of an organization and cascade downward through relevant other levels until sufficient execution is attained, we will provide the high-level view that emerges by beginning at the senior executive level (CEO) of the enterprise.

To explain Figure 4.7, we use the increasingly common scenario wherein organizations must produce not only acceptable financial performance and impacts to satisfy key stakeholders, but also socially equitable and environmentally sensitive performance. Impacts are demanded by citizens and regulatory agencies if not by our own consciences. Prior to examining Figure 4.7, we note that it is naïve to expect such positive "end of the pipe" *triple bottom line* (Elkington, 1997) performance and impacts without formulation of relevant "into the pipe" *triple top line* strategy (McDonough and Braungart, 2002).

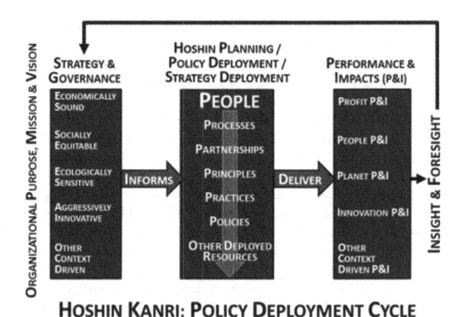

HOSHIN KANRI: POLICY DEPLOYMENT CYCLE

FIGURE 4.7
Hoshin planning from an enterprise perspective.

Examining Figure 4.7 from left to right, we see that most enterprises have clearly defined purpose, mission, and vision. The function of enterprise strategy and governance is to serve this purpose, vision, and mission. Contemporary enterprises increasingly strive to be economically sound, socially equitable, and ecologically sensitive and hence formulate their strategy accordingly, with many organizations also needing to incorporate other context-driven strategy elements, such as being aggressively innovative in order to compete or to remain or become relevant in the marketplace. Although a typical organization will have numerous strategies, the *Pareto Principle* (Juran, 2005) of separating the "vital few" (strategies) from the "trivial many" suggests that a few of these will be primary, that is, *hoshin* that populate the vital few, while the others will be relatively less important and will constitute the trivial many. Given the growth of triple top line approaches, and the importance of innovation, many organizations may have one or two *hoshin* that emerge from each of these categories.

Once executive level *hoshin* are determined, those executives will communicate these "*what to*" priorities on to the subsequent organizational level. Those responsible at the next level are provided with these *hoshin* or *whats*, generally with little to no guidance as to "*how to*" fulfill these: determination of *how* is up to those at that level, as is the selection of *which hoshin* are relevant to their span of influence. Those responsible at this next level will then determine the relevant *how-to* elements and these become the *hoshin* or *whats* that are cascaded to the following level.

This process continues, with the *hoshin* or *whats* at one level translated into *hows* at the next level until the plan is fully elaborated, transforming in the process from "big vision" to "execution." Relative to Figure 4.7, this process begins with strategy at the executive level seen on the left side of the Figure, and is unfolded through various levels, with people doing the unfolding through progressive translation of *whats* into *hows* into *whats* into *hows*, as represented by the center portion of Figure 4.7, ultimately delivering performance and impacts along the way as seen in the rightmost box of Figure 4.7. The mechanisms of the transformation are portrayed in the center portion of Figure 4.7: people, processes, partnerships, principles, practices, policies, and whatever other resources might be deployed/applied.

It is important to note that this is a living or cyclical process in that performance and impacts resulting from *hoshin* implementation are intended to provide both *insight* into recent enterprise performance and *foresight* into future enterprise priorities. Of course, it is also important for the organization to be externally aware so that future priorities might be influenced by new, pending, or likely legislation; by technological changes; by economic cycles; by emerging megatrends; or by other things not herein cited, but yet highly relevant to the enterprise's competitive landscape.

Seen in this context, *hoshin* planning can be regarded as analogous to application of Deming's Plan-Do-Study-Act (PDSA) Cycle at the enterprise level or, indeed, at whatever level *hoshin planning* is practiced (Moen and Norman, 2010).

Part 3: Hoshin Planning Applied

Illuminating examples of hoshin planning use by Western enterprises are abundant and readily available. For that reason, they are only briefly mentioned herein, accompanied by references where implementation details can be found. It would be erroneous to presume that *hoshin* planning is equally well implemented in all areas of a given enterprise, nevertheless, those cited are ones that have made fortuitous use of the method. In such instances, it is clear that enterprise-wide transparency has been a critical success factor: when the workforce understands corporate mission, vision, and purpose, they can better manage their own priorities and activities and appropriately adjust in order to better align these with enterprise goals, especially enterprise-level hoshin (Witcher and Chau, 2007).

Perhaps best known for use of hoshin planning among Western organizations are Xerox Corporation (Witcher and Butterworth, 1999) and Hewlett-Packard (Witcher and Butterworth, 2000). Of course, *hoshin* planning has use around the globe, with the initial apostles of *hoshin* planning commonly being global enterprises that have first experienced positive domestic results. As but a single example among many, we point to Nissan Corporation and their successful use of *hoshin* planning in their South African plant (Witcher, Chau, and Harding, 2008). Numerous early examples of transfer of *hoshin* planning and other significant Japanese management innovations can be found in, e.g., Kano (1993) and Lillrank (1995).

Climbing the Hoshin Planning Ladder: Nuts and Bolts Facilitation

Figure 4.7 presents a contextual view of *hoshin* planning's fit in the larger enterprise perspective, but does little to aid implementation, and it is to implementation that we now turn. Although implementation can be and usually is challenging, it can be fruitfully approached through a relatively concrete, almost algorithmic means. Given that the primary consumers of this contribution will have little or no experience with *hoshin* planning, our focus is on providing such an algorithmic, step-by-step approach. We begin by examining Figure 4.8 which provides an adaptation of a commonly used depiction of the *hoshin* planning process.

We see in Figure 4.8 that executive/senior leadership and management is responsible for the formation and communication of "big" vision and objectives to the following management tier, mid-level management, which in turn explicitly translates these into their strategy while also identifying and developing requisite resources that will be needed for deployment. This communication, represented by the two-way arrow connecting vision and objectives to strategy and resources, is a negotiated dialogue wherein explicit goals are set. In turn, mid-level management communicates their strategy and distributes resources to *hoshin* implementation teams that are responsible for determining precisely how and in what time horizon

FIGURE 4.8
The Hoshin planning process.

execution will take place. Negotiated dialogue or catchball between mid-level management and the implementation teams, represented by the two-way arrow between strategy and resources and activities and execution horizon, identifies and agrees upon the measures by which success or failure of a *hoshin* implementation is assessed. Similarly, executive/senior leadership and management review implementation team proposals to determine whether these are sufficiently aligned with vision and objectives and, of course, are sufficiently aggressive to meet strategic/competition critical needs.

As a final note on Figure 4.8, the arrowheads of varying size positioned on the *hoshin* planning cycle (that is, the outer circle of Figure 4.8) are intended to indicate two things: that *hoshin* planning is in fact cyclical, and further, that the time horizons generally differ. The large arrowhead on the right of Figure 4.8 indicates that executive/senior leadership and management often address longer horizons of three to five years, middle managers address shorter horizons of one to three years as indicated by the medium arrowhead at the base of Figure 4.8, and implementation teams routinely attend to activities with horizons of one year or less, as signified by the small arrowhead on the left side of Figure 4.8.

Figure 4.9 provides a commonly used *hoshin* planning tool that is referred to as an X-matrix.

Revealed in Figure 4.9 are executive/senior leadership and management breakthrough objectives (*hoshin*) at the bottom of the X-matrix, in relation

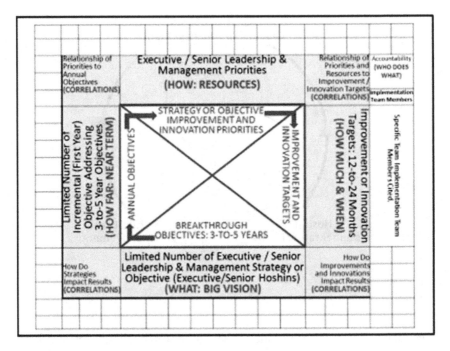

FIGURE 4.9
Hoshin planning X-Matrix.

to which are nearer-term objectives on the left side of the graph, with the relative strength of the relationships in the lower right-hand corner of the graph. Near-term objectives are in turn related to executive and senior leadership and management priorities that are reflected by dedicated resources as revealed at the top of the X-matrix, with the strength of relationships between the two provided in the upper-left corner of the X-matrix. Associated with dedicated resources are specific targeted outcomes that form the right side of the "X," where the relationships between priorities and targeted improvements and innovations are depicted in the upper-right corner of the X-matrix. Finally, we see on the extreme right side of the X-matrix specific efforts associated with specific implementation teams and team members. The relationships (correlations) cited in the four corners of the X-matrix are often symbolized as being strong, moderate, weak, or, in some instances, as an empty cell indicating no relationship between specific elements. Other context-driven elements may be added to the X-matrix as needed.

As a second useful aid in *hoshin* planning implementation, we cite the A3 tool (Chakravorty, 2009) where A3 refers to the size of paper commonly used, that is, 11 inches by 17 inches, or twice the size of standard US-letter format paper. A3 document content is often populated by steps associated with the plan-do-study-act or PDSA cycle, though we here recommend a modified PDSA cycle similar to the one provided in Figure 4.10 that is subsequently described.

Due to Walter A. Shewhart and popularized by Dr. W. Edwards Deming, the PDSA cycle is also referred to as the Deming Wheel or, more commonly, as the PDCA cycle, where the word "check" rather than "study" was used by Dr. Deming until later in his life. Toyota and many other companies make routine use of the PDSA cycle relative not only to *hoshin* planning, but as a general use problem-solving tool, including, often, in an A3 format (Shook, 2009).

Whether provided in an A3 or other format, the (modified) PDSA cycle of Figure 4.10 may be described as follows:

As with any journey on which one embarks, it is prudent to fully understand where the journey originates, that is, to *assess the current or baseline conditions*, including current performance levels and the root causes of inadequate performance (Doggett, 2005). Use of PDSA implies there is a gap between current and aspirational performance and,

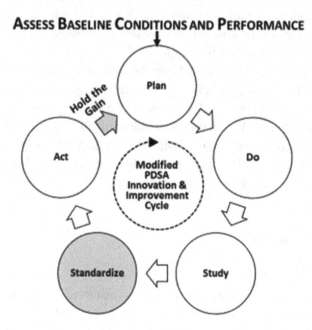

FIGURE 4.10
PDSA Cycle modified to include standardization and gain-holding.

generally, the decision has been made to pursue an incremental approach to improvement. Relevant to *hoshin* planning, it is appropriate to note that while executive and senior leadership and management *hoshin* correspond to "big vision," as *hoshin* planning cascades strategy through the enterprise, that at each successive level strategy transforms more and more into tactics which these increasingly corresponding to incremental change: PDSA cycles, in whatever format, are useful for anyone, at all levels.

Once the current situation has been assessed, the individual or team preparing the PDSA/A3 will *identify planned beneficial changes that address* the process or system under consideration, as well as the goal or target performance level resulting from those changes. This is followed by "doing" *(implementing) the planned changes*, potentially on a limited or pilot scale since changes may not prove sufficiently beneficial to warrant full-scale implementation. The status of the changed process or system will then be *assessed or studied* (that is, "checked") to document its new performance capability and whether the gap between prior performance and the goal or targeted performance has been adequately addressed. If the gap has been adequately addressed, the changes will be *standardized and fully documented* with the purpose of making the solution resulting from the changes a more portable one, at which point the solution will be fully implemented and process control established that ensure that benefits of the changes are maintained.

In noting that use of PDSA is typically cyclical, the individual or team responsible for the specific PDSA will likely engage in another round of planning, *ad infinitum* until the performance of the process or system in question is sufficient. We further note that while PDSA ordinarily pursues a series of incremental improvement that, collectively, yield large-scale improvement, use of PDSA does not preclude attainment of breakthrough improvement on any given iteration.

SUMMARY

Hoshin kanri is known by many names, including policy deployment, strategy deployment, and *hoshin* planning. Originating in Japan, the primary intention of *hoshin* planning is to translate strategy into actions that ultimately yield relevant performance and impacts. A number of tools and methods are available to support this process, but it is critical not to place undue focus on the tools, numerous variations, and adaptations of which can be found. Equally, it is important not to "fall in love" with a given strategy and to recognize that there is no perfect strategy, only better and worse ones; relevant, less relevant, and irrelevant ones.

Hoshin planning has been successfully used in many organizations, among them Bridgestone Tire—where *hoshin* planning originated—Toyota, Nissan, Hewlett-Packard, and Xerox. Although it is a highly structured strategic planning and deployment process, *hoshin* planning is versatile and can be of value to organizations in any business sector, including yours.

Create Constancy of Purpose

By Mark Baker*

When I was a young mechanical engineer at Honda Motor Company, Mr. Honda was still alive and he used to always say, "Unless we have 100% of the people in the organization engaged in making the company better, we will never be able to realize our true potential." I remember hearing this for the first time, and over the years I have found it to be a great insight, but the real question now is, how is this achieved? Mr. Honda's statement hits on two key points of building a successful organization, namely engagement and alignment. Without both of these aspects, success will be hit or miss.

The *Shingo Model*'s definition of the principle Create Constancy of Purpose is "an unwavering clarity of why the organization exists, where it is going, and how it will get there," which goes on to say, "enables people to align their actions, as well as to innovate, adapt, and take risks with greater confidence."

The principle of Create Constancy of Purpose lies in the Enterprise Alignment dimension of the *Shingo Model*. A consistent and clear purpose for an organization becomes the "why," which every individual in the organization uses to assure their energies and efforts are properly aligned. But it also should be much more than just a point of reference for alignment purposes. In order to truly transform an organization, the why must be powerful and move people at their deepest level. Of course, it is essential that leaders try not to create a new why every quarter or year,

---

* Mark Baker is a former Executive Director of the Shingo Institute.

but rather stick to the clear reason why the organization exists, even in challenging times.

One great example of this is at Autoliv, a tier-one automotive supplier of airbags and other safety systems. Autoliv's mission, "We Save Lives," is clearly and powerfully communicated everywhere you go in their organization, and people really believe it deeply. Of course, they have the typical banners, posters, and signs on the walls, but they also display pictures and videos of end-use customers whose lives have been saved by their products. These pictures are dramatic examples of how their product impacts the end-use customer. Many of these testimonials used on their walls and video monitors are of Autoliv employees and their families, really bringing the message home. But this isn't just a feel-good effort; they have been able to translate the why into actions. Each meeting at Autoliv involves the question, "What can I/we do to save more lives?" You can see it and feel it as you walk around and talk to people there.

Does having a clear and powerful why really matter? I answer with an emphatic "Yes, it makes all the difference!" Research shows that companies with engaged employees have five times higher shareholder returns than those that don't. If people feel good about the work their organization does, and if they feel they are valuable contributors to that good, they enjoy their work more, are energized by the work and find it rewarding, which all translates into better performance and results. Things always tend to go better when everyone in the organization is engaged and motivated to do the right things. However, we must always keep in mind that while engagement is important, engagement without alignment can be a frustrating failure for the group. Both engagement and alignment are needed in order to be successful in the end.

Even though leaders communicate the why clearly, if people in the organization consider it to be just the talk of leaders and not something leaders really believe, then it will not work. It is absolutely critical that leaders believe in the why, and show that they really believe, and are guided by it in their work too. If there is hypocrisy, employees will quickly sense it! Employees need to see and feel the genuineness of leaders in the purpose! As people feel that genuineness, they begin to accept it and believe in it themselves. It is important this why is truly embraced from the very top of the organization, all the way through each level (vertically) and division, function, and department (horizontally) in order to achieve real enterprise alignment at a deep cultural level.

Dr. Shingo said that know-how is not enough. People need what he called "know-why." By making sure you create constancy of purpose in your organization with a powerful and engaging why, you can set the stage for an incredible organizational transformation toward sustainable excellence and success!

Drowning in Opportunities

By Bruce Hamilton

In 1989, after four years of what could be called à la carte improvement, my factory was introduced to policy deployment by Deming Prize winner Ryuji Fukuda. Tossing a dozen Delta Airlines swizzle sticks on the glass of an overhead projector, Dr. Fukuda asked our team. "Does your plan look like this?" The shadow of the swizzle sticks pointing every which way created an impression.

In truth we had many plans—*too* many plans: There was a quality system to be installed, and a new computer system, and there were layout changes on the factory floor and in the office. There were new product plans and plans for new resources to build them. And finally, there were Lean-type initiatives to shorten lead-time and reduce cost. I used to joke, "We're drowning in opportunities. The problem is deciding what to do first."

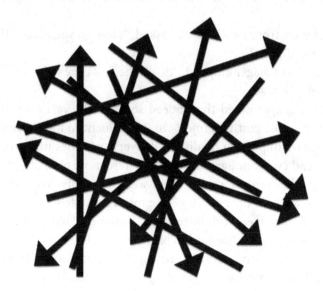

FIGURE 4.11
Dr. Fukuda's swizzle sticks.

Dr. Fukuda's projection however, suggested a bigger problem: Not only were there too many improvement projects vying for scarce resources, but there was a likelihood that without a unifying direction and method for alignment, certain projects would work at cross-purposes to others. Our discovery from the one-week workshop was that while each department thought it had clear marching orders, when the various plans were overlaid, they resembled Dr. Fukuda's swizzle sticks.

Today, I see a similar problem almost everywhere I go. Recently I gave a homework assignment to a client to list all key improvements on a single page. Two weeks later they sheepishly handed me sheet printed in six-point type. "It's the only way we could fit them on the page," they declared. The priorities were broken out by department.

"Why so many?" I asked. After some discussion, two chief reasons for the volume emerged:

1. Their quality system required them to identify areas annually for quality improvement. Owing to insufficient resources, few of these priorities could actually be addressed soon, but it was sufficient that they be identified. Many had been carried over from year to year.
2. Managers each received many additional objectives relating to cost or delivery. Like the departments they managed, the managers themselves were infinitely loaded down—drowning in opportunities.

Taking a page from Dr. Fukuda, I asked, "How do you know all of these priorities are aligned?"

"We don't," a manager quipped, "this is the first time we've seen them all together on one page."

Another manager noted that indeed some of the various projects *did* conflict. Some cost-cutting projects in department A, for example, would have a negative impact on quality or delivery priorities in a downstream function. And everyone agreed that there were more priorities than could possibly be addressed in a year. There were too many goals and too few means. "We work on the hot ones," one manager added.

"Too much manager-work-in-process," I replied, "like trying to fit ten pounds of potatoes in a five-pound bag."

"More like a *hundred* pounds," an engineer exclaimed, "I feel like I'm spending 5% of my time on twenty projects, and almost nothing gets done."

"How do we get out of this mess?" a top manager interjected.

I replied to her, "My own experience is that policy deployment isn't an overnight success. But it starts with the question you just asked. It's a new way of thinking that challenges the same mindsets as on the shop floor: push production, high inventory, and local efficiency. So, let's start by agreeing on what's most important to the customer and then aligning improvement projects regardless of department to the customer need. Then let's agree to limit the manager-work-in-process to enable these projects to flow."

"But how do we know what's *most* important to work on?" the top manager persisted.

I had asked Dr. Fukuda the very same question in 1989. So, I responded to her with the same answer Dr. Fukuda gave me:

"You're the manager!"

5

Results: Create Value for the Customer

Those who are not dissatisfied will never make any progress.

Shigeo Shingo*

The fourth and final dimension is Results. Great results are the outcome of following the principles that govern the results. The closer one emulates ideal behaviors, the closer one is to achieving enterprise excellence, consistently delivering ideal results to all stakeholders.

The focus of most leadership is on results, commonly called key performance indicators or KPIs. The principle in this dimension stresses that value needs to be considered from the perspective of the customer, rather than from that of enterprise leadership. All leaders of organizations share one common responsibility: they are responsible for results.

It is important to differentiate between leading and lagging indicators. Leading indicators are generally described as a behavior, whereas lagging indicators measure performance results. Therefore, the indicators used to influence and change behavior are generally different from, but connected to, the ones that report the results or KPIs on which leadership is measured. Please do not misunderstand what the Shingo Institute is advocating. The Institute understands that an organization must get results to succeed. They are simply saying that how one achieves the results is just as important as the result itself when it comes to sustainability and enterprise excellence.

Here are some testimonials that successful enterprise excellence companies have made about results:

---

* Shingo, S. *The Sayings of Shigeo Shingo: Key Strategies for Plant Improvement.* Cambridge, MA: Productivity Press, 1987.

Results are at the top of the pyramid for Shingo on their principles and it's extremely important and that's what we're all here about. So, everything in the rest of the Model is supporting the results. Customer forward is results, so that's really the key outcome of everything in the *Shingo Model*.

Rick Whitman, *Senior Lean Manufacturing Champion, Haworth, Grand Rapids, MI, US*

The results come. Instead of always focusing on dollars and savings, it's about focus on the people, external people—our customers—and internal staff. That drives the culture, that drives the results.

Morgan Jones, *Head of Group Productivity, Commonwealth Bank of Australia (CBA), Sydney, NSW, Australia*

CREATE VALUE FOR THE CUSTOMER

To satisfy the customer is the mission and purpose of every business.

Peter Drucker*

The focus of this principle is on creating value for all stakeholders. Ultimately, value must be defined through the lens of what a customer wants and is willing to pay for. Organizations that fail to deliver both effectively and efficiently on this most fundamental outcome cannot be sustained over the long run. If the customer does not feel value, the organization will lose the customer, and nothing else really matters.

We need to challenge everything we do and look at it through the eyes of the customer. As Dr. Shingo points out:

A relentless barrage of "whys" is the best way to prepare your mind to pierce the clouded veil of thinking caused by the status quo. Use it often.†

Create Value for the Customer means that every aspect of an organization should be focused on creating value for the customer. It is helpful to

---

* Drucker, P. F. *The Essential Drucker: The Best of Sixty Years of Peter Drucker's Essential Writings on Management.* New York, NY: Collins Business Essentials, 2008.

† Shingo, S. *Kaizen and the Art of Creative Thinking – The Scientific Thinking Mechanism.* Vancouver, WA: Enna Products Corporation and PCS Inc., 2007.

consider this a True North concept that should guide decision-making and continuous improvement. An organization needs to drive all aspects of value, including quality, cost, delivery, safety, and morale.

Many organizations assume that customer surveys tell them what their customers truly value. However, this approach has its limitations, and it is important to understand the difference between customer satisfaction and customer value as they are not the same thing. Customer satisfaction is essential, and unless it is met, we are unlikely to be able to have meaningful discussions about value. One way to look at this is that customer satisfaction looks backwards, i.e., it tells us how well we are doing against things we already do. Customer value, on the other hand, should look at what customers potentially value from us in the future.

A deep understanding of both customer satisfaction and customer value is critical to drive business excellence and innovation. It is important to link the understanding of customer value to strategy and have a system that deploys the understanding of customer value throughout the organization.

IS *CREATE VALUE FOR THE CUSTOMER* A PRINCIPLE?

In the ENTERPRISE ALIGNMENT workshop, the delegates are asked to explore the principle of Create Value for the Customer in order to deepen their understanding. The Shingo Institute uses several criteria to help delegates explore their understanding of this principle in more detail. The reader is encouraged to think about these criteria and consider their own answers. Each of these criteria is explored in more detail below. See Figure 5.1.

Create Value for the Customer

- What could we learn about this principle from studying the systems in your organizations?

- What are some of the current behaviors evident in your organization as they relate to this principle?

- How have those behaviors impacted your organization's culture?

- Think of both positive and negative behaviors?

FIGURE 5.1
Questions to Create Value for the Customer.

IS *CREATE VALUE FOR THE CUSTOMER* UNIVERSAL?

Does Create Value for the Customer apply to everything? It is useful to consider, why does any organization exist? Whether it is a nonprofit, a government department, a bank, a manufacturer, or a hospital, they all exist to deliver results to one type of customer or another. If those results are not of value, then the organization will ultimately cease to exist.

IS IT TIMELESS?

One way to think about this is to ask "Is there an end where this principle would not apply?" Can you think of any situation where at some point in time this principle would cease to apply?

DOES IT HAVE CONSEQUENCES?

Organizations that create value for their customers grow, and usually very successfully. It is possible to continue in the short- to medium-term not providing value, but growth is very unlikely and it is not sustainable over the long-term. Eventually, any organization that does not create value will cease to exist.

Some negative examples that can be observed when this principle is not applied include:

- High churn on customers with few repeat sales
- Negative customer reviews
- Low staff morale due to level of customer complaints
- A shrinking business
- A constant focus on cost-cutting

Where this principle is applied, we see the opposite of all the above, but in addition, some of the positive consequences are:

- Business growth with long-term customers.
- Customers are advocates for the organization.

- Employees have pride in the business.
- The organization has a great reputation and strong brand.

WHAT HAPPENS WHEN THIS PRINCIPLE IS OBSERVED?

In other words, think about what you would see in organizations where this principle is being applied. For example, it is highly likely that you will be able to observe some of the following:

- People at all levels talk positively about the customer.
- Lots of innovation and improvement activities focused on the customer.
- Established systems that embed the voice of the customer at all levels.
- Customer Value Propositions on all visual management boards.

5 WHYS

It can help to deepen our understanding of the principle by applying a 5 Whys analysis (see Figure 5.2).

It is useful to try and put this principle into your own context. Ask yourself why this principle is important to your organization. This is a good exercise to deepen understanding of the principle and its application

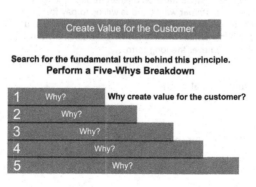

FIGURE 5.2
5 Whys: Create Value for the Customer.

to your organization and works well if undertaken by a cross-functional team.

The context and thus the answers for each organization will be different, but a generic example is given below.

1. Why is Create Value for the Customer of value to our organization?
   Answer: Because we need to give our customers what they value.
2. Why do we need to do that?
   Answer: Because if we don't do that, they will likely go to someone else who does or find a different way to get what they value.
3. Why does that matter?
   Answer: Because if this happens, the organization will eventually cease to exist and we will all be out of a job.

As Sam Walton, Founder of Wal-Mart, said:

There is only one boss: the customer. And he can fire everybody in the company from the chairman on down, simply by spending his money somewhere else.*

In summary, the Shingo Institute believes that Create Value for the Customer is important because (see Figure 5.3):

Create Value for the Customer

Business Case:
Ultimately, value must be defined through the lens of what a customer wants and is willing to pay for. Organizations that fail to deliver both effectively and efficiently on this most fundamental outcome cannot be sustained over the long-term.

Fundamental Truth:
Trust is Sacred.

FIGURE 5.3
Importance of Create Value for the Customer.

---

* Walton, S. and Huey, J. *Sam Walton, Made in America: My Story.* New York, NY: Doubleday, 1992.

WHAT IS CUSTOMER VALUE?

According to Womack and Jones,* the first Lean principle is to understand what customers value. At first, this may seem an obvious starting point for any organization wishing to be successful in whatever products or services they are seeking to supply. However, in reality, it is often overlooked, with organizations assuming they know what customers value.

Customer value is constantly changing and one of the models that helps describe this is from Professor Kano,† who divides value into three categories. These are illustrated in Figure 5.4 below:

Kano's model illustrates that customers only articulate basic value criteria when they are absent and that most often it is performance criteria that are expressed. Delighters that can help to inform future value are not readily articulated and need a structured process to help uncover them.

The Kano model helps to illustrate that what customers value changes over time and that expectations are constantly increasing. Today's delighter quickly becomes tomorrow's performance expectation, and the day after, a basic requirement. This is easily illustrated in a day-to-day example of computer technology, where today's delighter quickly becomes

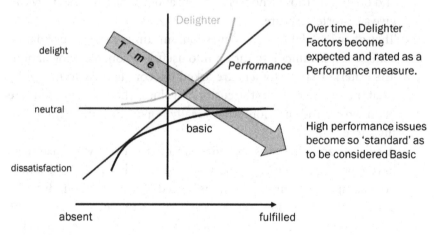

FIGURE 5.4
Customer Value (Adapted from Professor Noriaki Kano.)

---

* Jones, D.T. and Womack, J.P. *Lean Thinking: Banish Waste and Create Wealth in Your Corporation.* New York, NY: Simon & Schuster, 1996.
† Kano, N., Seraku, N., Takahashi, F. and Tsuji, S. Attractive Quality and Must-Be Quality. *Journal of the Japanese Society for Quality Control*, 1984. 14(2): 39–48.

a performance factor, then a basic, and then falls even further to have little or no value.

True customer value can only be understood by using a structured dialogue that focuses discussion on the future rather than just assessing historical performance.

This model helps explain why every organization needs to embed a culture of continuous improvement focused on customer value. Without this, the organization cannot thrive in the long-term, as their offerings become out of date.

So, what do we need to do to understand customer value? Customer surveys can be useful to give an indication of how we are performing today against a range of predetermined criteria. They are useful to collate feedback in a standard format and can give indications for areas of performance improvement.

There are, however, a number of dangers of relying on customer surveys to help understand customer value. These include:

- Surveys tend to look at historical performance, whereas customer value needs to look ahead at what customers value in the future.
- They are often completed by only a relatively small number of people and often only those who feel strongly about something, so they can give a distorted picture.
- They often have far too many questions, meaning that so much data is collected, it is difficult to turn it into useful, actionable information.
- The criteria that customers are asked to score is predetermined by what the supplier thinks the customer values. These assumptions are often wrong and therefore what's really important can be missed in the survey.
- A survey rarely helps us to understand the reasons why customers have scored criteria in a certain way, and as such, can be misleading. For example, customers may value "speed of response," but different customers' expectations can be wildly different. So, we may get low and high scores for the same question with the same level of service, making the results difficult to understand.

Increasingly, customer value is being referred to as "the Voice of the Customer" (VOC), and to truly understand the Voice of the Customer, organizations need to engage in a structured dialogue, rather than relying on static surveys.

The Voice of the Customer approach follows a number of key steps:

- Determine who the strategically important customers are to grow business with in the future.
- Identify the key stakeholders in those customers whose views on value are essential to understand.
- Undertake structured interviews with the key stakeholders using trained personnel to determine the vital few value criteria.
- Get insight from the customer on how current performance compares to their expectations against the value criteria they have said is important.
- Get insight into how the supplier compares to competitors against the value criteria.
- Get insight into how the supplier compares to the customer's best other supplier of anything at all.
- Collate and analyze the feedback.
- Build action plans to address the areas of opportunity and agree on review dates with the customer.

It is often a very useful exercise to get a range of managers in an organization to determine what they think their customers value and rate themselves against the criteria they have set. In many cases, it quickly becomes apparent to the managers that they are guessing. Comparing the actual feedback from the customer insight process to what the managers initially thought can be very enlightening for the management team.

It is possible to attain consistently high scores in customer satisfaction, but still lose work with a customer due to a failure to truly understand value. This was illustrated in the case of a manufacturer of electrical connectors who year on year achieved very high feedback scores on their customer satisfaction survey. Initially, there was some skepticism as to the need to undertake the Shingo Insight process, but this soon evaporated when the main customer revealed as part of the interview process that all future designs were based on wireless technology. At the time, all production and all products in development at the supplier were based on hardwire technology. Excellent customer value scores had lulled the supplier into a false sense of security, and they were in danger of becoming the best supplier of products the customer no longer needed. The Voice of the Customer work led to a rapid shift in strategic direction and product development activity.

One organization that has embedded Creating Value for the Customer as a key input to strategic goal setting is Airbus Australia Pacific. Their approach is shared in the case example below.

AIRBUS AUSTRALIA PACIFIC CASE STUDY

Chris Butterworth, Kim Gallant, and John Shapcott

A Lean culture requires us to understand the customer's needs and our VOC exercise has made those needs abundantly clear. We use the VOC to obtain a better understanding of our customer's expectations at the different levels at which they operate. What we aspire to are products and services that are inspired by our customers. To achieve this outcome, we go beyond the features or solutions they ask for to understand and then satisfy their underlying needs. The VOC exercise has already brought us closer together and we continue to drive operational improvements and efficiencies for the benefit of our customers.

Kim Gallant, *Manager Business Improvement and Operational Excellence, Australia Pacific*

Please note that some of the detailed findings have been left out of the case study for confidentiality reasons, with the main focus being on the process followed and the lessons learned.

THE ORGANIZATION

With more than 1,700 staff at 19 sites across Australia and New Zealand, Airbus Australia Pacific delivers new Airbus aircraft and supports more than 500 aircraft through a network of local facilities. The company is also assembling and supporting 22 ARH Tiger and 47 MRH90 helicopters for the Australian Army.

In addition, Airbus Australia Pacific maintains the Royal Australian Air Force's (RAAF) AP-3C Orion reconnaissance aircraft, C-130J Hercules. Through the work of subsidiary Safe Air, Airbus Australia Pacific supports the Royal New Zealand Air Force's C-130s and P3s while being recognized as a leader in propeller and engine maintenance.

Airbus Australia Pacific main customers in the defense sector have a well-established and rigorous performance scorecard system. This system reports achievement against agreed key performance indicators that are included in the contractual agreement. How each KPI is to be defined and reported on is agreed in detail and performance review meetings are held on a regular basis.

In 2011, Airbus decided that, while the scorecard system was very good, it gave limited understanding of the wider aspects of customer value. In effect, it is a very good mechanism for measuring customer satisfaction against current requirements, but provides little real insight into potential future needs.

Airbus therefore decided to engage their main customer in a detailed Voice of the Customer activity. The Voice of the Customer (VOC) is defined as "the stated and unstated customer wants, needs or requirements—expressed in the customer's own words." This information was critical to ensure Airbus met the current and future needs of their customers. The results of the VOC are used to ensure that the company Strategic Plan, and all subordinate plans, align with the requirements of our customers.

The findings from the 2011 work were of such value that Airbus decided to repeat the in-depth process every three years, with full VOC activity being undertaken in 2014 and again in 2017. One of the Business Improvement managers summed up his experience of the process:

Our Voice of the Customer projects have played a critical role in understanding what our customers truly value. We use the information gathered to drive our strategy, evolve our value streams, and target our improvement activities. It is a considerable investment of time and effort; however, it is well worth it, with our customers appreciating the opportunity to speak with us and ultimately both organizations benefit from the whole process.

John Shapcott, *Manager, Fixed Wing Business Improvement*

Regular reviews with the customer were undertaken after each VOC activity, but the three-year full review cycle worked well due to the contract lengths and the personnel posting cycles at the customer. Typically, the majority of customer personnel changed every three years on fixed posting cycles, so three years allowed for new people to settle into their roles. The work was also used to inform future strategic planning.

VOC OBJECTIVES

From the start of the process, it was essential to be clear on the objectives, not just with the customer, but also internally. This is summed up neatly by Martin Ball, one of the Airbus Vice Presidents:

> We have commenced our third VOC cycle within the Fixed Wing business and the information has once again proven invaluable in helping us understand what our customers value, and equally important, what they don't value. This information is vital input into our strategic planning process and business operations. It informs and instills confidence in our strategy. In the highly competitive aerospace environment in which we operate, we will continue to conduct VOC activities to ensure we achieve what is most important to grow into the future—delivering excellent outcomes to our customers and Airbus Australia Pacific.

The specific objectives were modified over the three cycles, but were broadly similar. The objectives of the 2017 VOC activity were:

1. To obtain a better understanding of customers' expectations at the different levels in which they operate.
2. Gather data to better inform how they communicate with customers.
3. Identify gaps in how they perform against customer needs.
4. Set in place strategies to close any expectation gaps that exist and modify Strategic Plans accordingly.
5. Drive operational improvements and efficiencies.

Airbus wanted to ensure that their services were inspired by their customers, rather than the answer being designed and predetermined by the customer. To achieve this outcome, the discussions were designed to go beyond the features or solutions the customers asked for and instead sought to understand and then satisfy the underlying needs.

THE PROCESS

In order to do this, a simple 5-stage process was established as shown below:

Stage 1: Confirm Purpose of the VOC

The key was to involve and engage internal senior level sponsors and stakeholders to align on objectives. Once this was completed, the team approached the key contacts at the customer to agree on the process and agree on shared objectives.

The objectives agreed upon included:

- Gather data to better inform how they communicate with customers.
- Identify gaps in how they perform against customer needs.
- Set in place strategies to close any expectation gaps that exist and modify Airbus Strategic Plans accordingly.
- Drive operational improvements and efficiencies.

Stage 2: Collect VOC Data

The first step was to identify who the key stakeholders were at the customer and agree on the objectives and timing with them. Customers were usually interviewed individually, with most interview sessions typically taking 45–50 minutes. Preparation for the interviews was critical and clear roles and responsibilities were agreed by the interview teams along with an agreed process.

Stage 3: Analyze and Report VOC Data

Following the interviews, the data was compiled and analyzed using a structured process as outlined below:

1. Extract Customer Need statements and transcribe to "Post-it" notes.
2. Color-code Post-it notes by customer segment.
3. Group and sort customer needs using the "affinity" technique.
4. Identify and highlight the "Top Needs" from each customer.
5. Construct a Critical to Quality (CTQ) tree diagram to highlight the "Top Needs" for each program based on an approved weighting.
6. Evaluate and extract customer views on Airbus performance utilizing the assessed questions.
7. Produce tables highlighting the segmented customer assessment of Airbus performance.

Stage 4: Build an Operational Metrics Dashboard aligned with Contract Metrics, the Customer Experience, and Strategy Scorecard

Stage 5: Identify and Close Gaps principally using Lean Six Sigma projects and Relationship Management initiatives

---

RESULTS

One of the most insightful pieces of information that became apparent through reviewing the 2017 VOC results compared to the 2011 and 2014 results was that the whole nature of the relationship between Airbus and the customer had changed. The initial VOC activity in 2011 generated a lot of feedback on transactional and contractual compliance activities. The 2014 results showed a clear strengthening of the relationship, with a positive shift to discussions of a much wider range of topics. The 2017 results showed an even greater strengthening of the relationship, with discussions moving to long-term strategic collaboration opportunities and exploration of options that had previously not even been considered.

As a result of undertaking the VOC activity, one example of the benefits achieved is that Airbus and the customer are actively collaborating with joint cross-functional teams. These teams use a structured Practical Problem-Solving methodology to analyze agreed issues and opportunities and implement shared solutions.

A good illustration of this is the example of typical feedback that was obtained as a result of undertaking the VOC activity from an Airbus Australia Pacific customer:

I'm currently living an availability dream for C-130Js and that's because of the teamwork and relationship we have with Airbus Group AP. I know I can go in directly and touch the provider if I'm either satisfied or dissatisfied and I get an immediate response to it. So, to me, whilst there is a contract in writing, there is also a contracting relationship and that's what I value out of your organization—you recognize that there is a contract, but you will go beyond that and value the relationship you have with Defence. And I'm not just saying that, I mean it.

AIRCDRE W. McDonald,
Commander Air Mobility Group, Royal Australian Air Force

BEHAVIORAL BENCHMARKS

The Shingo Institute believes that the understanding of this principle can be deepened by considering what is referred to as "behavioral benchmarks." These are intended to help us look at the principle from many different perspectives and act as a guide or reference point to help define behaviors that support this principle. It is not the intention that the application of this principle is limited to only these behavioral benchmarks, as it's important to remember that the context of every organization is unique. However, they provide a very useful basis for further discussion and exploration of the principle. The behavioral benchmarks for Create Value for the Customer are Relationships, Value, and Measures, and these are explored in more detail below.

Relationships: We build relationships with our customers to meet and anticipate their needs and align our objectives to them.

Jeff Bezos, founder and CEO of Amazon, strongly believes in the importance of customer relationships:

> We see our customers as invited guests to a party, and we are the hosts. It's our job every day to make every important aspect of the customer experience a little bit better.*

Building strong customer relationships is critical to business success. The probability of selling to existing customers is shown to be many times higher than the probability of selling to new customers and is a fraction of the cost. This list is not exhaustive, but some of the key elements of building strong long-term relationships include:

- Actively listening to what customers are saying. Make sure you understand their feedback and never dismiss this.
- Help your customers to be successful by making your success their success.
- Don't focus on the dollar per minute of any transaction, but rather on the value of the whole account.
- Ensure that goals and objectives are aligned to those things that are important to the customer.

---

* Bishop, T. Jeff Bezos explains why Amazon doesn't really care about its competitors. *Geekwire*, September 17, 2013. Available at www.geekwire.com/2013/interview-jeff-bezos-explains-amazon-focus-competitors/.

Tony Hsieh, founder and CEO of Zappos, also emphasizes the importance of customer relationships in the success of his business:

> We take most of the money that we could have spent on paid advertising and instead put it back into the customer experience. Then we let the customers be our marketing.*

In other words, he seeks to provide such great service that customers become advocates for his business. There are no better sales people than your own customers.

EXAMPLES OF IDEAL BEHAVIORS

Some example of behaviors that support the behavioral benchmark of Relationships are given in Table 5.1.

Some potential KBIs for Relationships are given below:

- Rating system of percentage of employees that state they have strong positive relationships with peers and customers (may be internal)
- Percentage of customers' contacts on regular random checks that highly rate the relationship
- Customer satisfaction metrics

TABLE 5.1

Relationship Behaviors

Create Value for the Customer: Relationships	Example Behavior
Leader	Frequently asks questions to ensure that people understand the importance of positive relationships with colleagues and customers
Manager	Demonstrates and proactively encourages collaborative relationships across their team and across departments and customers
Associate	Seeks to build and maintain strong collaborative relationships with all colleagues and customers

---

* Hsieh, T. *Delivering Happiness: A Path to Profits, Passion, and Purpose.* New York, NY: Business Plus, 2010.

Value: We investigate what our customers really value and communicate that through the whole organization.

Bill Gates, founder and former CEO of Microsoft, speaks to taking the negatives and turning them into positives for your company:

Your most unhappy customers are your greatest source of learning.*

The best assumption that one can make about customer value is that you don't know what it is. Too often we impose our own perspective of what the customer values, only to find that they value something completely different. One company the editor came across was about to implement a cost-saving to the way that one of their main product lines was packed in shipping. The editor was taking a site tour accompanying one of the company's key customers. On the tour, the customer noticed by chance some of the product had been packed in the new way. The resulting conversation once back at the offices was a bit of a surprise to the supplier.

Customer: "Many thanks for the tour. That was interesting. I noticed that you have some product [x] packed in a different way than we have been receiving it for the last couple years."

Supplier: "Yes. We have developed a much more efficient way of configuring the packaging and shipping will start in the next day or so of the new pack."

Customer: "Has anyone checked with our team about the change?"

Supplier: "Um. Well, no. I mean, we haven't changed the product at all. Just the way it is loaded onto the pallet. We didn't see that it would make any difference to anyone else."

Customer: "Well, it does. That new configuration won't fit into our front-end machine. We would have to adjust every pack before we could use it. You do realize that the main reason we buy from you is that the way you pack is perfect for our machine configuration? If you send it to us like that, we won't be able to use it."

Supplier: "Oh. Ok, we didn't realize that. We will get together with your team ASAP, and in the meantime, we will make sure we only ship the old packaging configuration."

---

* Gates, B. *Business @ the Speed of Thought: Succeeding in the Digital Economy.* New York, NY: Warner Books, Inc., 2000.

Another example of the difficulty of understanding customer value is that standard terms are often interpreted in very different ways. One such example is "response time." For some people, a response time of 24 hours is fine; for others, it may be a couple of days. For some people, it might be less than one hour. It may even depend on the type of communication (e.g., phone, email, etc.) and/or the type of issue requiring a response. But what's true every time is that the response time requirement will be an expectation by the customer. Often it might not even be explained—they will expect you to know. The only way to find out for sure is to talk to them.

A useful tool to consider is sometimes called the "customer value proposition." In other words, have we clearly defined what it is the customers really value from the product or service we are providing? Earlier in the chapter, we discussed the voice of the customer activity, and the customer value proposition is a good way to summarize what the customer really values into a simple one-page statement. For example, it is very powerful to do this between teams internally. The key to making this work is that it can only be constructed as a result of discussion with the customer. It should never be written up assuming we know what the customer values. Ideally, it is jointly drafted with the customer, and as a minimum, it is signed off by them. It can then be used to inform metrics and targets and decision-making. Good practice is to have it on prominent display on the teams' visual management board.

The customer value proposition needs to be constantly reviewed with the customer, as their expectations, and hence what they value, will change rapidly over time. As such, we need to develop systems that not only capture the voice of the customer, but have mechanisms that take feedback and make constant adjustments to the way we understand and take actions informed by customer value.

Elon Musk, former CEO of PayPal, SpaceX Founder, and current CEO of Tesla, believes in the power of feedback:

> I think it's very important to have a feedback loop, where you're constantly thinking about what you've done and how you could be doing it better.[*]

One of the criticisms that is often levelled against the Voice of the Customer and CVP approach is that customers don't know what they value. To support this assertion, a famous quotation attributed widely to Henry

---

[*] Ulanoff, L. Interview with Elon Musk. *Mashable*, April 13, 2012. Available at https://mashable. com/2012/04/13/elon-musk-secrets-of-effectiveness/?europe=true#6mVDYwVyQaqh.

Ford is often used: "If I'd asked my customers what they want, they would have said faster horses."

This is misleading. Although there is doubt that Ford actually said this, what Ford implicitly understood was that what his customers valued was time. They wanted to get from A to B as fast as possible. The key to understanding customer value is not to focus on what the customer wants (e.g., a particular solution—faster horses), but to focus instead on the need they are seeking to address (e.g., travel time).

A similar argument is put forward about Apple. While there is undoubtedly a need for technology push, lots of technology fails to get traction because it does not address a customer need. It's true that no one ever said, "I want an iPod" before Apple brought them to market. But many people expressed a desire to be able to listen to music while they were jogging.

A good question for any team and even every individual to ask themselves is "Who is the customer?"

Although the traditional view of customers as end users, or as a chain of immediate recipients of a product or service en route toward an end user, may be appropriate in some contexts, this view is often too narrow. In the context of the *Shingo Model*, the concept of customers may be expanded to include multiple relevant stakeholders that may span the supply and value chains and beyond. This view will address the needs, wants, and sensitivities of producers or providers; users, consumers, or recipients of products and services; and those directly or indirectly impacted by the manufacture, distribution, use, or provision of a product or service, including individuals, civil society, policy makers, and the natural environment. This view requires a balancing of stakeholder considerations and is consistent with increasing expectations that enterprises should be both socially and environmentally responsible.

Some examples of behaviors that support the behavioral benchmark of Value are given in Table 5.2.

Some potential KBIs for Value are given below:

- Percentage of employees on random checks that are advocates for customer value
- Percentage of employees on random checks that can explain customer value
- Percentage of employees on random checks that can explain what they are doing to increase value for the customer

TABLE 5.2

Value Behaviors

Create Value for the Customer: Value	Example Behavior
Leader	Frequently asks questions about customer value to reinforce people's understanding
Manager	Ensures that customer value information and feedback is regularly updated and understood by the team
Associate	Informs day-to-day decision-making by reference to the customer value proposition

Measures: We measure to know where we are in relation to our objectives.

Not everything that can be counted counts, and not everything that counts can be counted.

William Bruce Cameron*

Unfortunately, many organizations will often measure what they can rather than what they should. What they measure should be directly related to what the customer values. One of the best ways to deploy customer value down through any organization is to make sure people understand:

- How what is being measured links directly to the customer
- Why it is important to the customer
- How the target supports the customer's requirements

ABC STEEL MILL CASE STUDY

One example of this is a steel mill the editor visited several years ago. The mill painted steel in a wide variety of different colors for use in the construction industry. The voice of the customer activity revealed that

---

* Cameron, B. *Informal Sociology: A Casual Introduction to Sociological Thinking.* New York, NY: Random House, 1963.

key value criteria for the customers was lead time from order to dispatch. Further analysis and discussion revealed that if a lead time of one week could be achieved, then the company could win a lot more orders compared to the competition, who were generally offering a four-week lead time. Initial ideas on how to do this included massively increasing inventory, but this proved to be prohibitively expensive. So instead, a cross-functional team was set the task of coming up with ideas on how to hit a one-week lead time. This resulted in a recommendation to create enough capacity to be able to paint every color every week if needed. In order to do this, the key constraint was the changeover time between colors, which needed to be reduced by some 80%. Clearly this was not an easy thing to do, but the whole organization set about trying to achieve it. On one visit, the editor noticed some of the associates videoing each other. Intrigued, he asked them to explain what they were doing.

Associates: "We are videoing how we perform this part of the changeover so that we can work out how to reduce it."

Editor: "Why do you want to reduce it?"

Associates: "If we can get our part of the changeover down to under three minutes, it means we can support the overall target of being able to paint every color every week."

Editor: "Why do you want to paint every color every week?"

Associates: "Because if we can do that, we can offer a one-week lead time to the customer and we can beat [xxx] (their main competitor) and win more work."

It took a few months, but eventually a one-week lead time was offered on all major colors and the order book grew significantly.

YOU GET WHAT YOU MEASURE

Measures will drive behavior. To paraphrase Eli Goldratt, "Tell me what you are measuring and I'll tell you what result you are seeing."*

---

* Goldratt, E. M. and Cox, J. *The Goal: A Process of Ongoing Improvement.* Great Barrington, MA: North River Press, 1984.

Several years ago, the editor was visiting a logistics company who were regretting introducing a new bonus system for their drivers.

Logistics Company Manager: "We thought the bonus system was a great idea. We wanted to reduce the amount of fuel we use, as it's one of our major costs, and we also thought that it would be a good way to support our environmental policy."

Editor: "Sounds like a good idea."

Logistics Company Manager: "Yes, we thought so. Every driver now gets a bonus based on fuel efficiency. The more kilometers they do with less fuel, the higher their bonus. It's calculated in such a way that the company still saves money even with the bonus payment."

Editor: "But it's not working?"

Logistics Company Manager: "No. It's been a complete disaster. We just didn't realize what behavior the system would cause. You see, the simplest way to save fuel is to drive slower, which is no bad thing. But we have people driving excessively slow, resulting in the deliveries arriving late. One of our biggest contracts is with a major supermarket and we have to pay penalty charges for every late delivery. Our penalty charges from customers have gone through the roof under the system, as we are making lots of late deliveries, but the drivers still get their bonus."

Editor: "Oh dear."

Logistics Company Manager: "Exactly. And that's not all. The other way to get really good fuel consumption is to drive an empty truck. Occasionally, drivers might not be able to pick up the return load for a genuine reason and have to return to the depot with an empty truck. However, the number of instances of no return load being available have doubled since we introduced the bonus and our truck utilization has plummeted."

Editor: "Sounds like it's a real headache."

Logistics Company Manager: "Yes, and today was the final straw. A fight broke out between two drivers because one accused the other of trying to siphon off some of his fuel so that he could get a bigger bonus. They've all gone mad!"

The bonus system was reviewed and changed once the unexpected impact on behavior was understood.

One way to think about measures is to "measure what matters." Historically, measurement has been focused on management—what management needed to know to be able to plan, organize, and control. Within a model where widespread involvement is essential for continuous improvement and consistent performance, it is important to define measures that matter to those who will use them and can be directly linked to what the customer values. Therefore, associates need different measures than leaders responsible for the overall enterprise. Many thought leaders on measurement have suggested the new measurements need to:

1. Directly tie to strategic priorities; move the dial,
2. Be simple and easy to capture,
3. Give timely feedback that is tied to the cycle of work, and
4. Drive improvement.

Measures that matter can be created throughout the organization to assure that everyone is focused on the appropriate strategic activities and driving continuous improvement that moves the whole enterprise ahead.

Some other key checks for measures include:

- Measures must drive the required behaviors.
- The best measures tell us what's happening, not what's happened, i.e., there should be some leading indicators in combination with lagging indicators.
- The measure must be the right measure for the people doing the work, i.e., they must be able to influence it.
- All measures must have targets that make sense to people and are clearly linked to the business goals.

Even when we think we are measuring the right thing, we can often come up against the law of unexpected consequences. For example, one of the things that's important in supermarkets is to have accurate stock records. To help support this, many supermarkets have teams of stock checkers whose job it is to count actual stock and record any discrepancies. This is one way of picking up "stock losses" or "shoplifting" by customers. The cost of this job is recognized as a waste and a lot of effort is put into reducing the need to do it, but also make it as efficient as possible. To help achieve this, people in the role are often given daily targets for the number of items they need to count. Unfortunately, if they are running behind target and can't find something

TABLE 5.3

Measures Behaviors

Create Value for the Customer: Measures	Example Behavior
Leader	Ensures that any targets on measures are clearly linked to business goals and customer value and the "why" is clear
Manager	Proactively reviews measures in a Plan, Do, Check, Act cycle and adjusts quickly as needed
Associate	Regularly highlights and challenges measures that are making it difficult to live the ideal behaviors

quickly, it is much easier to record a stock loss and move on to the next item on the list. This efficiency measure often leads to incorrect stock "write-offs" and a lot of rework. It is essential to apply Plan, Do, Check, Act to any measure and be prepared to change it when it isn't driving the desired behavior.

Some example of behaviors that support the behavioral benchmark of Measures are given in Table 5.3.

Some potential KBIs for Measures are given below:

- Percentage of employees that say the way they are measured drives the ideal behaviors
- Percentage of teams that have KPIs directly linked to customer value on their VMB
- Percentage of employees on random checks that can give examples of how a measure has impacted their customer in the last month

SYSTEMS

As the *Shingo Model* demonstrates, systems drive behavior, so it is important to ensure that systems are constantly reviewed and refined to support and encourage the desired behavior. One of the key high-level systems associated with the principle Create Value for the Customer is Voice of the Customer. Some of the main elements that need to be included in this system are given below:

- Customer visits are frequent.
- Associates are commonly sent to the customer site to understand how their product or service is used.

- Associates receive direct feedback from the customer.
- Feedback is received and sought from the customer visits.
- There is a structured process for gathering customer data.
- Feedback from the customer is frequent and in real time.
- Customer expectations are clear and visual.
- Principles help align systems to select appropriate tools to drive desired behavior and achieve customer expectations.
- Customer feedback is shared rapidly to all levels of the organization.
- Measures are used to drive improvement.
- Feedback from customers is visual and in use to make improvements.
- Improvement activities demonstrate a clear understanding of customer feedback received.
- Improvements are being made based on customer satisfaction facts and data.
- Associates know which current and future improvements are tied directly to increasing customer satisfaction.
- Customer satisfaction is considered while prioritizing improvement activities.

SICHUAN TOYOTA CASE STUDY: CREATE VALUE FOR THE CUSTOMER

Introduction

While Ritsuo Shingo was at Sichuan Toyota, he worked with different dealers to improve their sales and often visited them to understand how they could improve. When visiting a dealer in Xi'an in June, he met with one of their potential customers. The customer wanted to buy 25 Coasters by the end of July, as there was a new highway that would be completed at the end of July. The customer wanted to drive a fleet of new Coasters to celebrate the new road. However, the lead time was too short for the plant to deliver 25 new Coasters; they could only make 12 Coasters in that timeframe. Shingo called the managers of each Toyota dealer and asked if they had any Coasters to send to Xi'an. Between the plant and the dealers, they were able to meet the goal. They had to drive the Coasters to Xi'an, more than 15 hours from Chengdu, and they arrived in Xi'an one day before the opening of the new highway.

Create Value for the Customer

Definition

It is important to create value for all stakeholders. Ultimately, value must be determined by what a customer wants and is willing to pay for. Organizations that fail to deliver both effectively and efficiently on value cannot be sustained in the long run. If the customer does not feel value of the product or service, you will lose the customer, and nothing else really matters.

Tools

Shingo believed in a *model of maximum output with minimum input* in all areas of the business, from plant construction to daily expenses. He adjusted budgets constantly to ensure there were no wasted assets.

Examples

Thrifty Office Supplies: When Ritsuo Shingo was at Sichuan Toyota, he strove to be cost-conscious when purchasing office supplies and to instill a cost-conscious mentality in the employees. For his company car, he could have ordered a new, medium-size car, but he asked the Toyota Beijing office to send him a used car. This spread to the Chinese partner of Sichuan Toyota. Mr. Cheng, the Chinese general manager, elected to buy small, cheap cars for the general managers instead of buying new mid-sized cars. The cost-conscious mentality also spread to the purchase of office furniture. Shingo found his desk and chair at a used furniture market. Mr. Cheng told him he thought they would fall apart quickly. After seeing Shingo's desk, Mr. Cheng went to the same used furniture market and was able to find brand new desks that were obtained in a plant's bankruptcy. This saved the company about $60/330 yen per desk. Mr. Cheng then took the initiative to be cost-conscious when purchasing computers for the company. He researched three different suppliers and proposed purchasing them from a Taiwanese supplier, since the specifications were acceptable and the price was the cheapest. This saved Sichuan Toyota money by purchasing the cheapest computer that worked for their needs, rather than buying the top-of-the-line models.

Jiuzhaigou National Park: The Jiuzhaigou National Park only allows park-operated mini-buses to drive in the park, which has hundreds of miles of roads. There is no Toyota dealer near the park, so it was open territory for new dealers. Ritsuo Shingo convinced the Chengdu Toyota dealer to drive some Coasters more than ten hours to give park customers the opportunity to test drive them. The dealer had to drive over a mountain range of 3,500 meters/11,500 feet with no guardrails and the risk of plunging down the mountainside. Shingo and the dealer met with the president of a sightseeing company, who was also in charge of the Environmental Protection Agency in that area. The sightseeing company wanted vehicles with natural gas engines for environmental reasons, but Coasters were not made with them. The sightseeing company declined to purchase Coasters during the visit; however, several months later, the company decided to buy 25 Coasters because they had more visitors to the park than they expected. Shingo offered to drive them out, but the company picked them up and loaded the Coasters with electrical appliances. Eventually the sightseeing company ordered over 100 Coasters (Figure 5.5).

Guangqi-Hino Plant: When Ritsuo Shingo was head of Hino China, they formed a partnership to establish Guangqi-Hino, which manufactured heavy-duty trucks. They considered many different locations for the new plant in Guangzhou, but wanted to be respectful of a Toyota plant on the south side of the city. Shingo wanted the plant far away from the Toyota plant, as the wages at the Hino plant would be lower than the Toyota plant and the Toyota supplier plants in the area, making it difficult to hire good

FIGURE 5.5
Nuorlang Waterfall in Jiuzhaigou National Park.

workers if the plants were close together. They found a location in a small city on the north side of Guangzhou with no manufacturing plants nearby, which helped build the city's economy. The Chinese partners wanted the office section of the plant to be beautiful with an expensive fence and garden. Shingo convinced the Chinese team to use cheaper materials, saving the company 3 million yen.

Daqing Oil: One of Hino Motors' biggest customers was Daqing Oil, located in Daqing, the largest oil field in China. Daqing Oil was using 80 Hino trucks in their oil field operations, in addition to competitor trucks. Daqing Oil made several requests for help in improving Hino trucks. Shingo visited the company to assess the situation and how best to meet their needs. After his visit, he sent engineers who were able to implement most of the improvements they needed. Through their visits, Shingo was able to convince Daqing to continue purchasing trucks from Hino.

Toyota Training Center: While Ritsuo Shingo worked at the Toyota Training Center, he sent reports to Mr. T., the chairman of Toyota, reporting any problems at a dealer or supplier. He found the chain to report and fix problems at the dealer or supplier was quite long and difficult to maneuver. He reported this issue to Mr. T. and explained it was important to find a quick solution to problems he found. Toyota sent field quality engineers to the Toyota Training Center, and they were able to resolve field quality problems much quicker than previously.

RESULTS

Examples of Shingo's Successes

World Record at Sichuan: Shingo set a goal in 1990 to set a world record at the Sichuan plant. He wanted to make a profit in the plant's first business year, which hadn't ever been done at a Toyota overseas plant. He posted the slogan in each department, but Mr. Liu, the vice president of the Chinese joint venture company, didn't like it because city officials didn't think it was achievable and would cause trouble. Mr. Liu was afraid of getting fired. The signs were taken down by employees, but Shingo did not abandon the goal. He looked for ways to save money and worked hard to sell Coasters. The goal was achieved and they set a world record. They continued to make a profit for more than ten years in a row.

Beijing Airport: Shingo found it is important to be open to new possibilities and new markets. While selling Coasters at Sichuan Toyota, Shingo met with the management team at the Beijing airport and they ordered four Coasters. This initial sale opened doors for Toyota and they have sold Coasters in almost every airport in China. Shingo found that once he earned a good reputation, he could win a lot of business.

Dealer in Shenzhen: A dealer in Shenzhen was struggling with Coaster sales because the dealer usually waited for customers to come to him. Ritsuo Shingo met with him and suggested he take the Coasters to the customer. Shingo challenged them to sell more than 100 Coasters in one year, and then he would take the dealer's team to Jiuzhaigou from Chengdu if they met the goal. The dealership employees changed their approach, became one of the top three dealers in China, and surpassed the goal of selling 100 Coasters per year (Figure 5.6).

Shanghai Traveling Company: A dealer in Shanghai had a customer, Shanghai Traveling Company, who wanted to buy Coasters but wanted different tires on them first. Ritsuo Shingo personally visited the Shanghai Traveling Company and explained why the tires Toyota selected for the Coasters were better, that they had developed these tires for many years especially for the Coasters. Shingo said the Shanghai Traveling Company could come to him with any problems with the Coasters and he would make it right. The company bought nine Coasters after Shingo's visit.

FIGURE 5.6
Shingo with dealer in Shenzhen.

TABLE 5.4

Numbers for Creating Value

Creating Value for Customers in Numbers
• Saved $60/300 yen per desk by purchasing desks for Sichuan Toyota from used furniture market
• Saved money by purchasing smaller, cheaper cars for Sichuan Toyota company cars
• Helped Toyota dealers adjust their sales techniques, which increased sales
• Created key connections in government when selecting the site for Guangqi-Hino plant, which stimulated the economy and created new jobs in the area
• Retained Daqing Oil as a customer and created future business with them
• Solved problems quicker by bringing engineers on-site to Toyota Training Center
• Set a world record by being profitable the first year at Sichuan Toyota

DISCUSSION

Think about the products and services your organization provides. What value do these bring to customers? What needs to be changed to improve the value, which in turn would improve sales and revenue?

Value is not only creating quality product, but also at a low cost. Reducing business expenses enabled Toyota to sell product at a lower rate. How can you emulate Shingo's philosophy of saving money on business expenses to create value?

6

Lean Prescription at Denver Health: The ENTERPRISE ALIGNMENT Workshop Case Study

The ENTERPRISE ALIGNMENT & RESULTS workshop contains a case study highlighting the dimension of Enterprise Alignment. This is reproduced here, and the reader is invited to review it and identify examples of the application of the principles.

We decided on Lean because it was a philosophy as well as a tool set, and everyone could understand it. The philosophy was built on respect for people and continuous improvement. What was brilliant about the philosophy is that it links disrespect to waste. Waste is disrespectful to our patients because it asks them to endure processes with no value ....

Lean is about transformation. Certainly, it does improve quality and it does reduce cost. But the key component is that leadership must be involved. If leadership is not engaged, then forget it. Lean is so interesting because it requires the senior leaders to be heavily engaged, but it lets the frontline solve the problem.

Dr. Patricia A. Gabow*

---

* Patricia A. Gabow, MD, MACP was the CEO of Denver Health from 1992 until her retirement in 2012. Denver Health's Lean transformation earned the Shingo Bronze Medallion in 2011. Before inducing such a transformation, Dr. Gabow was a practicing nephrologist and academic researcher, serving as chief of nephrology, director of medical services, and chief medical officer at Denver Health.

THE CHALLENGE

The American healthcare system is filled with redundant and often conflicting regulations which burden patients, providers, and payers, as well as creating waste. Americans who should benefit from this system instead struggle with high cost, poor quality, and unequal access.

Huge Cost: So how expensive is the current healthcare system? Financially, it's a black hole. According to the Commonwealth Fund Commission on a High Performing Health System (2013), America spends twice as much on healthcare per capita than other developed countries. "Over the last four decades the growth in healthcare costs exceeded the GDP rate of growth in 31 of the 40 years," as cited in Dr. Patricia Gabow's book with Philip Goodman[*], *The Lean Prescription: Powerful Medicine for Our Ailing Healthcare System.*[†] Healthcare now consumes 18% of the GDP,[‡] with a total bill of approximately $3 trillion dollars. This substantial sum interferes with the United States' ability to invest in other priorities such as education, environment, or infrastructure. It also interferes with the United States' ability to reduce its federal deficit and improve its competitiveness in the global marketplace. Lastly, the Institute of Medicine has estimated that 30–40% of the total sum is waste. At today's expenditure level, this adds up to over 1 trillion dollars per year. This staggering amount does not benefit the patient or even the healthcare industry in the slightest. This financial waste is accompanied by inefficient, non-patient-centered clinical and administrative processes. As a result, the actual amount of waste more than likely greatly supersedes this fiscal amount.[§]

Quality Chasm: Despite the staggering cost, an optimist may conclude that the United States must get excellent healthcare as a result of this financial burden. However, studies have shown that as many as 251,000

---

[*] Philip L. Goodman, MS, RRT was the director of the Lean Systems Improvement Department at Denver Health, where he was employed from 1979 until his retirement in 2013. Mr. Goodman was responsible for overseeing Lean facilities and Lean educational programs and led the operational aspects of the Lean transformation effort.

[†] Gabow, P. A. and Goodman, P. L. *The Lean Prescription: Powerful Medicine for Our Ailing Healthcare System.* Boca Raton, FL: CRC Press, 2015, 2.

[‡] Commonwealth Fund Commission on a High Performing Health System, 2013.

[§] Gabow, P. A. and Goodman, P. L. *The Lean Prescription: Powerful Medicine for Our Ailing Healthcare System.* Boca Raton, FL: CRC Press, 2015, 3.

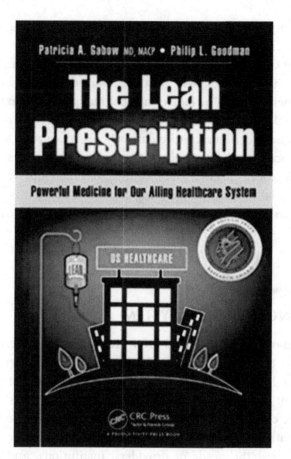

FIGURE 6.1
The Lean Prescription.

people died annually from hospital error.* Additionally, the Rand Corporation reported that Americans only receive about 50% of the care they need, and as much as 30% receive what is not needed, or even harmful.

Unequal Access: Those left out on the current healthcare structure continue to be the patients. Prior to the Affordable Care Act of 2010 (ACA), approximately 50 million Americans were without health insurance, according to the Kaiser Family Foundation (2014). Many Americans without healthcare have substantial barriers to accessing healthcare, and even those with private healthcare have high deductible co-payments when

---

* *British Medical Journal*, 2016.

they do attempt to access care. These overwhelming financial burdens are a significant cause of bankruptcy in the United States.

Prevailing Culture: A trip to the doctor's office will often consist of an extensive wait period, followed by a brief period with the doctor before essentially being done. The look of most clinics gives face to this culture: time is wasted here. Rather than increasing the effectiveness of the system, companies add televisions, couches, playsets, and magazines to better keep people distracted or occupied. No matter the tricks and distractions, going to see the doctor results in a lot of waiting, and therefore wasted time, as well as financial waste and increasing healthcare costs. It is obvious that the healthcare system is not designed with the patient's time or money in mind.

CHANGING TO A NEW SYSTEM

Patricia Gabow, the CEO for Denver Health, decided there needed to be a change. She was a successful leader, and while Denver Health was not a struggling organization, she realized there was still room for improvement and she went about doing just that. Her first step was to focus on the customer, in the belief that the customer defined value. This was a revolutionary concept for the healthcare industry that has largely evolved to meet the needs of providers, institutions, and regulations. While there are many "customers" which a hospital may need to address (pharmacy, suppliers, billing departments, etc.), Denver Health sought to put the patient at the center.

Once the patient was in focus, Dr. Gabow turned her attention to the systems in place and to the reduction of waste in regard to the delivery of value to her customers. A large piece of this step was to standardize and solve problems. Initially this standardization and focus on eliminating waste seemed to counter what she, and the medical industry, had in mind when creating systems—the intuitive idea of "batching" work, or more of an assembly-line type of organization. However, when tested, she discovered that one-piece flow was more efficient, such as in triage, trauma, and cardiopulmonary resuscitation. In these instances, teams can "deliver value on demand without waste with structure, practice, and discipline in circumstances when we know effective flow means patient survival."* This realization highlighted the reality that either medical professionals do not see the value in reducing waste in more routine processes, or the routine healthcare processes are too complicated to see the flow in the processes.

Dr. Gabow focused the next piece of her improvement process on creating clear goals and transparency. After some focused prioritizing with the executive team, value streams were created. "These areas reflect the organization's core business but they are narrow enough to provide focus."† Dr. Gabow imagined this value stream (VS) like a real stream which flows smoothly to the ocean with limited boulders and rapids to slow it down. Her goal was to eliminate these boulders (barriers), essentially minimizing or eliminating non-value steps. To keep on a focused path, Denver Health began with 5 VSs and increased this to 14 by the following year.

With these targeted VSs in place, it was time to start asking why. Focusing on the success of Toyota and their 5 Whys, Dr. Gabow implemented these questioning strategies and observations to take a clearer look at the waste and processes currently in place in her departments. During "waste walks," teams of observers would receive a list of "wastes" and be instructed to observe them. One such observation method includes mapping the path involved in getting a job done. Such mapping can lead to improved workplace design and streamlining of systems.

Dr. Gabow discovered many tools such as these to help map and identify wastes in her hospital. Now that she had identified areas that needed improvement, she needed to get a team together to help drive that improvement.

Realizing that expert help was needed, a Lean systems improvement department was created, with a mix of internal and external employees and using reclaimed positions from some of the existing revenue improvements. From this platform, a training program was created. Without the budget to send employees to Japan to be immersed in Lean, Denver Health opted for a more basic four-hour training session for executive staff and physician directors, and a smaller group of 25 handpicked, eager, and respected

* Gabow, P. A. and Goodman, P. L. *The Lean Prescription: Powerful Medicine for Our Ailing Healthcare System.* Boca Raton, FL: CRC Press, 2015, 30.

† Gabow, P. A. and Goodman, P. L. *The Lean Prescription: Powerful Medicine for Our Ailing Healthcare System.* Boca Raton, FL: CRC Press, 2015, 36.

administrators and mid-managers to become the first "black belts." This group received 48 hours of Lean training. The initial training was done with external instructors, but over time, Denver Health created their own training program and ran two courses each year. These black belts were asked to use Lean and eliminate waste in their day-to-day activities and were reviewed monthly. After four years, they were tasked with eliminating $30,000 in waste that fiscal year.

The process of eliminating waste became fun. Employees began working together to identify and eliminate wastes, essentially making their jobs easier. In one instance, simply upgrading a janitor's mop fabric to microfiber saved water, chemical usage, and employee steps, all the while improving mopping time by 15%. In the laboratory department, the employees worked so hard to improve their wasted workspace that the accreditation inspector believed they had undergone a department remodel. In the respiratory therapy department, a scavenger hunt to find 20 randomly selected items decreased from 14.4 minutes to 8.7 minutes after using the 5S method and eliminating waste. That is a 40% reduction in time, physical steps, and frustration in looking for items, with an increased focus on patient care. That reduction translates to saved money and improved customer interaction and treatment.

Ultimately, implementing Lean practices did eliminate waste for Denver Health, but when the charts and facts are compiled, how does one identify and classify financial benefit? Is it dollars expended of revenue received? Also, what is the intended outcome? If money is saved, will departments have access to that money? Additionally, if processes are improved, will employees no longer be needed? Fortunately, at Denver Health, layoffs were not on the agenda; instead, small monetary bonuses were given as team awards when they proved financial savings or improvements. More than 600 employees received awards for their efforts with Lean.

In 2012, the black belts and 13 of the 16 VSs exceeded their financial targets, some by quite a large margin. The overall target for financial benefit was $35.7 million, and the actual impact exceeded more than $51 million. That is in addition to $120 million the previous four years.

Of course, as was discussed earlier, the goal was to focus on the patient—the customer—and increase value. While financial improvements are obviously good for the company, what impacts did the patients see? Throughout this process, many of the quality outcomes were aligned to national benchmark data instead of being linked to particular value streams. However, it is important to note that these broad measurements improved with the Lean efforts.

7

Assessing the Enterprise Alignment and Results Dimensions

The more deeply leaders, managers, and associates understand the principles of operational excellence and the more perfectly systems are aligned to reinforce ideal behavior, the greater the probability of creating a sustainable culture of excellence where achieving ideal results is the norm rather than the aspiration. This is what the Shingo Model *illustrates.*

The Shingo Institute

PREPARATIONS TO GO & OBSERVE

A key element of all the Shingo courses is to undertake a "learning by doing" activity to practice and embed the learning with a Go & Observe exercise. It's time to walk through the Go & Observe process. Here is a step-by-step process to consider:

Step 1: Decide on which of the three principles discussed in the book to focus on. Use the examples given in this book to inform the ideal behaviors that you want to see in your own organization. Have a go at writing these in your own words in the context of your organization using the template at Figure 7.1.

Step 2: Start to fill in the sheet shown in Figure 7.2, which is a copy of the assessment sheet. Across the top of the sheet, identify the area for observation (the physical location in the facility), the focus of the Go & Observe activity (i.e., which principle to work on), and the round

Principle:	Ideal Behavior:
Leader	
Manager	
Associate	

FIGURE 7.1
Principle study template.

Assessment Notes

SYSTEMS

AREA:	FOCUS:	ROUND:

IDEAL BEHAVIOR   OBSERVED BEHAVIOR

1 _____   1 _____
2 _____   2 _____
3 _____   3 _____
4 _____   4 _____
5 _____   5 _____
6 _____   6 _____
7 _____   7 _____
8 _____   8 _____
9 _____   9 _____
10   10

KEY QUESTIONS   · Create a series of tool, system and principle questions to ask.

1 _____
2 _____
3 _____
4 _____
5 _____
6 _____
7 _____
8 _____
9 _____
10 _____

FIGURE 7.2
Assessment notes template.

(the first time you do this, versus the second or the third, etc.). In the upper left-hand block, list the ideal behaviors to study.

The middle left-hand box is used to list the systems in your organization that you think will be involved in creating the behaviors

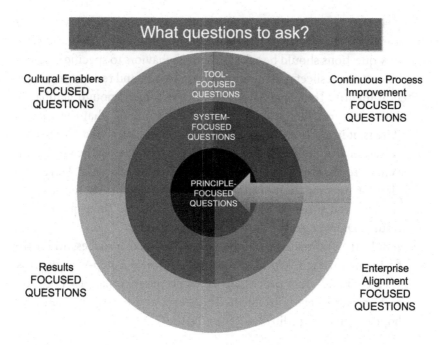

FIGURE 7.3
Constructing focused questions.

one will both observe and hope to find. Across the bottom of the sheet, list a set of questions to answer and identify, with the hope that the answers to these questions will provide an understanding of this principle or the behaviors one is looking for.

Figure 7.3 shows graphically how the questions should be constructed, concentrating first on Tool-Focused questions, which are the easiest for associates to respond to, then moving upward, searching for the systems responsible for the behaviors observed using System-Focused questions, and then connecting this to principles by identifying Principle-Focused questions.

Step 3: Engage in a Go & Observe (gemba). Go out and make the observations using the sheet shown in Figure 7.2. During the Go & Observe, you will fill out and change everything on the sheet. Learn as much as you can about the set of behaviors studied. In the gemba, do not go as a group and simply stand there and listen to the team leader. Instead, split up and talk to the actual people doing the work. Observe what is really going on. Seek answers to the questions listed on the sheet. The purpose of questions in the gemba are to help you identify evidence of the actual behaviors of leaders, managers, and associates.

Step 4: Repeat. Go back as a team and reconvene. Share what was learned. Find out what questions have not been answered and what new questions should be asked. Tie the behaviors to specific systems. Fill out a new sheet with new questions. Go out and repeat the gemba.

Step 5: Identify the gaps. After you have executed enough gembas to where you feel you have a clear understanding of what the current state is, it is a good time to reflect on the ideal state, and have a conversation around how to get from the current state to the ideal state. What are the gaps? What systems need to be changed? Develop a plan for the execution of those changes. Gain approval to make the changes and press forward implementing them. Then observe the results. Did you get the desired shift in behavior?

Step 6: Learn and try again. Rarely does one make a successful hit the first time through. Working toward the ideal is a step-wise process. It's a trial-and-error process. There is no manual that gives the correct answer to every problem. Try, learn, and try again, each time hopefully moving a little closer to the ideal.

THE SHINGO ASSESSMENT PROCESS

There is a lot to learn from an external assessment and the best ones will be principle-focused rather than tool-focused. The Shingo Institute recommends the Shingo Insight Assessment process, because it directly focuses on the *Shingo Guiding Principles* and gives the surveyed company a tool that will allow them to have insight to their shortcomings.

For more details about the Shingo Insight Assessment process, please visit https://shingo.org/insight.

THE SHINGO PRIZE AS AN ASSESSMENT TOOL

Another form of assessment that is utilized by a large number of companies is the Shingo Prize assessment process. The Shingo Prize has become the world's highest standard for enterprise excellence. As an effective way to benchmark progress toward enterprise excellence, organizations throughout the world may apply and challenge for this Prize. Recipients receiving this recognition fall into three categories:

1. Shingo Bronze Medallion
2. Shingo Silver Medallion
3. Shingo Prize

Most organizations do not wait until they believe they might qualify for the Shingo Prize to challenge. They challenge for the Prize so they can have a team of enterprise excellence experts visit their company and evaluate their performance. They see it as highly valued expertise at a low cost.

For more information about the Prize, and to see the hundreds of companies who have challenged for and received the Prize, visit shingo.org/awards. It is also useful to visit the Shingo Institute website to learn more about the Shingo Prize assessment criteria. Go to https:shingo.org/challengefortheprize, scroll down the page, and click the "Application Guidelines" tab to download the guidelines and assessment criteria.

8

Summary

In the editor's experience, many organizations struggle to truly deploy their strategy. No single leader or senior leadership team can deliver a strategy on their own. In order for the strategy to succeed, they need the help of the entire workforce. It is not unusual to see very good strategies fail because they have not been effectively deployed. Unfortunately, this often leads to an even greater focus on more and more communications, or in some cases, a rewrite of the "failed" strategy.

Too often senior leaders can be heard to make statements such as: "But I've told them the strategy twenty times and they still don't get it." It is not enough to tell people the strategy. At best, this will achieve communication of the strategy, and people may be able to recite back some elements of it. It will not, however, deploy the strategy, as people will not understand what it means to them and what they need to do to support it. The only way to ensure this is to deeply embed the principles of Create a Constancy of Purpose and Think Systemically.

When these principles are embedded, people are able to understand how their daily activities directly impact the strategic goals and how to choose the most important priorities in their workload.

When the principle of Create Value for the Customer is also embedded, the people throughout the organization will also understand the "why" behind the strategy. They will be able to align and connect with a common purpose and shared understanding of their role in achieving that purpose.

These three principles work hand-in-hand to truly deploy strategy linked to creating value for the customer. In an organization where these principles are applied well, people are:

- Aligned vertically up and down the organization on a common purpose

- Working collaboratively across departmental boundaries along customer value streams
- Able to understand what the strategic goals are, how they contribute to them, and why they are important to the customer and organization

This book has been written to accompany the Shingo ENTERPRISE ALIGNMENT & RESULTS workshop. A lot of the richness and learning in these workshops comes from the experience-sharing not just of the facilitators, but more importantly, the other delegates. Every time the editor facilitates one of these workshops, he learns something new. Hopefully this book will be of use to the reader as a stand-alone text, but if you have the opportunity to attend a workshop as well, it is highly recommended.

Bibliography

Ackoff, R. L. The Future of Operational Research is Past. *The Journal of the Operational Research Society*, 1979. 30: 93–104.

Adams, S. *Dogbert's Top Secret Management Handbook*. New York, NY: HarperBusiness, 1996.

Bishop, T. Jeff Bezos Explains Why Amazon Doesn't Really Care about Its Competitors. *Geekwire*, September 17, 2013. Available at www.geekwire.com/2013/interview-jeff-bezos-explains-amazon-focus-competitors/.

Butterworth, C., Harder, B. and Jones, M. *4+1: Embedding a Culture of Continuous Improvement in Financial Services*. Cartridge Family, 2017.

Cameron, B. *Informal Sociology: A Casual Introduction to Sociological Thinking*. New York, NY: Random House, 1963.

Chakravorty, S. S. Process Improvement: Using Toyota's A3 Reports. *The Quality Management Journal*, 2009. 16(4): 7–26.

Conti, T., Kondo, Y. and Watson, G. H. *Quality into the 21st Century: Perspectives on Quality and Competitiveness for Sustained Performance*. Milwaukee, WI: ASQ Quality Press, 2003.

Crawford-Mason, C. and Dobyns, L. *Thinking about Quality: Progress, Wisdom, and the Deming Philosophy*. New York, NY: Random House Value Publishing, 1998.

Daly, A. and Finnigan, K. *Thinking and Acting Systemically: Improving School Districts Under Pressure*. Washington, D.C.: American Educational Research Association, 2016.

Deming, W. E. Dr. Deming's 14 Points of Management. The W. Edwards Deming Institute, 2018. Available at https://deming.org/explore/fourteen-points.

Deming, W. E. W. Edwards Deming Quotes. The W. Edwards Deming Institute, 2018. Available at http://quotes.deming.org/authors/W._Edwards_Deming/quote/10091.

Doggett, A. M. Root Cause Analysis: A Framework for Tool Selection. *Quality Management Journal*, 2005. 12(4): 34–45.

Drucker, P. F. *The Essential Drucker: The Best of Sixty Years of Peter Drucker's Essential Writings on Management*. New York, NY: Collins Business Essentials, 2008.

Elkington, J. *Cannibals with Forks: The Triple Bottom Line of 21st Century Business*. Oxford, UK: Capstone Publishing, 1997.

Found, P., Griffiths, G., Harrison, R. and Hines, P. *Staying Lean: Thriving, Not Just Surviving*. Cardiff, UK: Lean Enterprise Research Centre, Cardiff University, 2008.

Gabow, P. A. and Goodman, P. L. *The Lean Prescription: Powerful Medicine for Our Ailing Healthcare System*. Boca Raton, FL: CRC Press, 2015.

Gates, B. *Business @ the Speed of Thought: Succeeding in the Digital Economy*. New York, NY: Warner Books, Inc., 2000.

Goldratt, E. M. and Cox, J. *The Goal: A Process of Ongoing Improvement*. Great Barrington, MA: North River Press, 1984.

Greenwood, R. G. Management by Objectives: As Developed by Peter Drucker, Assisted by Harold Smiddy. *The Academy of Management Review*, 1981. 6(2): 225–230.

Harris, V. *A Book of Five Rings by Miyamoto Musashi (1645)*, translated by V. Harris. Woodstock, NY: Overlook Press, 1982.

Hibino, S. and Nadler, G. *Breakthrough Thinking: The Seven Principles of Creative Problem Solving*. Rocklin, CA: Prima Publishing, 1998.

Hines, P. What Would Happen If...? *The Shingo Blog*, April 15, 2015. Available at https://blog.shingo.org/2015/04/what-would-happen-if/.

Howardell, D. Lean People for a Lean Enterprise. *The ACA Group*, January 1, 2011. Available at www.theacagroup.com/lean-people-for-a-lean-enterprise/.

Hsieh, T. *Delivering Happiness: A Path to Profits, Passion, and Purpose*. New York, NY: Business Plus, 2010.

Humes, J. The Art of Communication is the Language of Leadership. *International Trade*. March 27, 2008. Available at http://www.freshbusinessthinking.com/the-art-of-communication-is-the-language-of-leadership/.

Hutchins, D. *Hoshin Kanri: The Strategic Approach to Continuous Improvement*. Hampshire, UK: Gower Publishing Ltd, 2008.

Imai, M. *Kaizen: The Key to Japan's Competitive Success*. New York, NY: McGraw-Hill Publishing, 1986.

Jones, D. T. and Womack, J. P. *Lean Thinking: Banish Waste and Create Wealth in Your Corporation*. New York, NY: Simon & Schuster, 1996.

Jones, D. T., Womack, J., and Roos, D. *The Machine That Changed the World*. New York, NY: Simon and Schuster, 1990.

Juran, J. M. Pareto, L., Cournot, B., Juran et al. *Joseph M. Juran: Critical Evaluations in Business and Management*, 2005. 1(4): 47.

Kano, N. A. Perspective on Quality Activities in American Firms. *California Management Review*, 1993. 35(3): 12–31.

Kano, N., Seraku, N., Takahashi, F. and Tsuji, S. Attractive Quality and Must-Be Quality. *Journal of the Japanese Society for Quality Control*, 1984. 14(2): 39–48.

Kaplan, R. S. and Norton, D. P. *The Balanced Scorecard: Translating Strategy into Action*. Boston, MA: Harvard Business School Press, 1996.

Kondo, Y. Hoshin Kanri: A Participative Way of Quality Management in Japan. *The TQM Magazine*, 1998. 10(6): 425–431.

Lee, R. G. and Dale, B. G. Policy Deployment: An Examination of the Theory. *International Journal of Quality and Reliability Management*, 1998. 15(5): 520–540.

Liker, J. *The Toyota Way: 14 Management Principles from the World's Greatest Manufacturer*. New York, NY: McGraw-Hill, 2004.

Lillrank, P. The Transfer of Management Innovations from Japan. *Organization Studies*, 1995. 16(6): 971–989.

McDonough, W. and Braungart, M. Design for the Triple Top Line: New Tools for Sustainable Commerce. *Corporate Environmental Strategy*, 2002. 9(3): 251–258.

Moen, R. and Norman, C. Circling Back: Clearing Up Myths about the Deming Cycle and Seeing How It Keeps Evolving. *Quality Progress*, 2006. 43(11): 22–28.

Mr. Disraeli at Sydenham. *The Times*, June 25, 1872.

Mumford, T. Cultural Strata Effects: How Lean Culture Drivers of Engagement Vary by Employees' Level in the Organization. Shingo European Conference, December 2, 2016, Copenhagen, Denmark.

Nemo, J. What a NASA Janitor Can Teach Us about Living a Bigger Life. *The Business Journals*, December 23, 2014. Available at www.bizjournals.com/bizjournals/how-to/growth-strategies/2014/12/what-a-nasa-janitor-can-teach-us.html.

O'Neill, K. *Lessons from Los Gatos: How Working at a Start-up Called Netflix Made Me a Better Entrepreneur*. Seattle, WA: Amazon Digital Services LLC, 2014.

Perry, B. D. and Szalavitz, M. *The Boy Who Was Raised as a Dog: And Other Stories from a Child Psychiatrist's Notebook—What Traumatized Children Can Teach Us about Loss, Love, and Healing*. New York, NY: Basic Books, 2017.

Platt, S. *Respectfully Quoted: A Dictionary of Quotations Requested from the Congressional Research Service*. Washington, D.C.: Library of Congress, 1989.

Raiffa, H. *The Art and Science of Negotiation*. Cambridge, MA: Belknap Press of Harvard University Press, 1982.

Ramirez Resendiz, J. F. Beliefs and Systems Drive Behavior. *The Shingo Blog*, April 29, 2015. Available at https://blog.shingo.org/2015/04/beliefs-and-systems-drive-be havior/.

Schonberger, R. J. *World Class Manufacturing: The Lessons of Simplicity Applied*. New York, NY: The Free Press, 1986.

Schumacher, E. F. Work in a Sane Society. *Schumacher Center*, January 1972. Available at https://centerforneweconomics.org/publications/work-in-a-sane-society/.

Senge, P. M. *The Fifth Discipline: The Art and Practice of the Learning Organization*. New York, NY: Doubleday/Currency, 1990.

Shingo, S. *Kaizen and the Art of Creative Thinking – The Scientific Thinking Mechanism*. Vancouver, WA: Enna Products Corporation and PCS Inc., 2007.

Shingo, S. *The Sayings of Shigeo Shingo: Key Strategies for Plant Improvement*. Cambridge, MA: Productivity Press, 1987.

Shook, J. Toyota's Secret: The A3 Report. *MIT Sloan Management Review*, 2009. 50(4): 30–33.

Stevens, T. Dr. Deming: 'Management Today Does Not Know What Its Job Is' (Part 2). *Industry Week*, January 17, 1994. Available at www.industryweek.com/quality/dr-deming-management-today-does-not-know-what-its-job-part-2.

Sussland, W. A. Connecting the Planners and the Doers. *Quality Progress*, 2002. 35(6): 55–61.

Taylor, F. W. *Scientific Management, Comprising Shop Management: The Principles of Scientific Management and Testimony before the Special House Committee*. New York, NY: Harper & Row, 1911.

Tennant, C. and Roberts, P. Hoshin Kanri: Implementing the Catchball Process. *Long Range Planning*, 2001. 34(3): 287–308.

Ulanoff, L. Interview with Elon Musk. *Mashable*, April 13, 2012. Available at https://ma shable.com/2012/04/13/elon-musk-secrets-of-effectiveness/?europe=true#6mVDY wVyQaqh.

Walton, S. and Huey, J. *Sam Walton, Made in America: My Story*. New York, NY: Doubleday, 1992.

Whyte, W. H. Is Anybody Listening? *Fortune*, September 1950.

Williams, B. and Hummelbrunner, R. *Systems Concepts in Action: A Practitioner's Toolkit*. Stanford, CA: Stanford University Press, 2010.

Witcher, B. J. Policy Management of Strategy (Hoshin Kanri). *Strategic Change*, 2003. 12(2): 83–94.

Witcher, B. J. and Butterworth, R. Hoshin Kanri: How Xerox Manages. *Long Range Planning*, 1999. 32(3): 323–332.

Witcher, B. J. and Butterworth, R. Hoshin Kanri at Hewlett-Packard. *Journal of General Management*, 2000. 75(4): 70–85.

Witcher, B. J. and Chau, V. S. Balanced Scorecard and Hoshin Kanri: Dynamic Capabilities for Managing Strategic Fit. *Management Decision*, 2007. 45(3): 518–538.

Witcher, B. J., Chau, V. S. and Harding, P. Dynamic Capabilities: Top Executive Audits and Hoshin Kanri at Nissan South Africa. *International Journal of Operations and Production Management*, 2008. 28(6): 540–561.

Index

Printed in the United States
by Baker & Taylor Publisher Services